CRICKET
Yesterday & Today

This is a Carlton Book

First published in 2012 by Carlton Books
20 Mortimer Street, London, W1T 3JW

10 9 8 7 6 5 4 3 2 1

Text and design © Carlton Books Limited 2012

A CIP catalogue record for this book is available
from the British Library.

ISBN 13: 978-1-78097-115-5

Senior Project Editor: Matthew Lowing
Art Direction: Luke Griffin
Designer: Harj Ghundale
Production: Maria Petalidou
Picture Research: Paul Langan
Editorial: Jane Donovan, Shaun Barrington
& David Ballheimer

Printed in China

England's Geoff Boycott drives for Yorkshire in the
1970 Roses match at Old Trafford, squeezing the
ball past the outstretched hand of bowler David
Hughes. Boycs was eventually out for 98.

CRICKET
Yesterday & Today

Ian Valentine

CARLTON

Contents

Foreword by Kevin Pietersen MBE

Cricket has been a part of my life for more years than I care to remember and it has brought me joy, pleasure and excitement, but more than anything else an appreciation of a truly fantastic sport. It has given me the chance to travel the world, and to meet and play with and against some of the greatest sportsmen of the era.

In addition to that, cricket has given me some fantastic times and allowed me to make friends with many wonderful people. There is something unique about the camaraderie of cricket. In Test matches, you are face to face with an opponent for five days solidly and it breeds a trust and respect that can't be found in just 90 minutes.

Cricket Yesterday & Today is a wonderful book, showing cricket as it was in days gone by and the way it is today. Looking through the pages I simultaneously saw how much the sport has changed and actually remains the same as it ever was.

As well as the fantastic photographs, the essays that accompany each of the 95 topics help me realise how lucky I have been to spend my life in this fantastic sport. Any cricket fan, young or old, will find this a beautiful addition to their library.

Above: Spectators queue outside The Oval in 1938 for the first day of Surrey's match against the touring Australians.

Below: Seventy years on and cricket fans are still lining up alongside the red brick walls of The Oval, on this occasion for the first day of the fifth Test of the 2009 Ashes.

Introduction

Many thanks indeed for reading this book, the latest in the *Yesterday & Today* series. The wonderful selection of pictures illustrates just how much the game – and society, fashion, technology, photography for that matter - has transformed over the last 150 years.

The stout-bellied W.G. Grace in flannel breeks and neckerchief bears scant resemblance to today's ultra-fit T20 athletes in eye-sore acrylics, although the wily old doctor would have loved the big hitting and big bucks. Indeed, limited overs cricket has evolved at breakneck speed from even 15 years ago. Who knows how it will look in 2020?

Many of the nuances that have evolved the sport – safety equipment, technology, pitch preparation, law interpretation – are presented in the following pages. Yet, it's not all about change. Test cricket has largely stayed true to its Victorian roots, whether batsmen's scores and averages, a bowler's speeds and deliveries, the importance of brilliant fielding, or the fallibility of umpires. A hundred or a five-for is just as worthy now as it was in 1877.

Who doesn't enjoy hypothesising about yesteryear's heroes? Surely trailblazers such as Fred Spofforth, Victor Trumper, Clem Hill, Sydney Barnes, Ranji would have had the physical and mental abilities to make a living in today's game; but would they be modern superstars? Could Jack Hobbs have adapted his skills to T20? Should Sachin Tendulkar rate higher than Don Bradman, despite a vastly inferior batting average? How would Kevin Pietersen's technique have held up against Bill O'Reilly or Ray Lindwall? We can never know for sure, but it's fun to speculate.

And we should not view the past with too sympathetic a gaze. The black and white footage often paints a scene of simple endeavour and fair play, but cricketers have been trying it on since the first ball was bowled. Controversy has always loomed over the players like Father Time himself.

It could be that reinvention is more common in cricket than outright change. Perhaps that's why the sport enjoys an enduring appeal. The age-old urge to hit a ball with a bat and score more runs than the opposition remains the same. It's just that every generation moves the boundaries to suit modern tastes.

This book has been a great pleasure to research and write. I hope you enjoy its gentle stroll down memory lane, and back again.

One
The Players

Denis Compton (front) and Bill Edrich are cheered by a
vast throng at The Oval in 1953, after crowd favourite
Compton had struck the boundary that beat Australia in
the final Test and won the the Ashes for England.

1921

Inspirational Captaincy

Captains can lead in different ways, but example is one of the finest formulas. Scoring a hatful of runs like Don Bradman or Viv Richards immediately gains team-mates' support. Doggedness and fearlessness were attributes Allan Border and Mike Atherton could demand from their troops, both having them in spades. Respect is a vital ingredient – could West Indians Frank Worrell and Clive Lloyd have demanded such high standards were their own not stratospheric, too?

Strong leadership brings out the best in players. England's Andrew Strauss, for example, enjoyed a rich vein of form upon assuming the captaincy, while Australia's Michael Clarke started his tenure for Australia with a hatful of runs. Meanwhile, Pakistan's Misbah-ul-Haq is emerging as the calm presence his country needs.

Some of the greatest captains were worthy of a team place despite modest contributions with bat or ball. For those in favour of the scheming Scot, Douglas Jardine was the effective captain who couldn't buy a run for himself during the Bodyline Series. He offered to step down as a result, but his team voted for him to stay on.

Mike Brearley ended his England career without a Test century, but he is remembered as one of the finest strategic captains. His return to captaincy sparked the dramatic turnaround of the 1981 Ashes, albeit deposed skipper Ian Botham played a part.

Left: Australian captain Warwick Armstrong walks out with confidence at Trent Bridge in 1921, having whitewashed England 5-0 the previous winter Down Under. His side would win the next three Tests too.

Right: Wily Sri Lankan captain Arjuna Ranatunga is hugged by Muttiah Muralitharan after winning the 1996 World Cup final against Australia. His shrewd tactics often earned his side an advantage.

1964

Great Accumulators

Statistics don't always tell the full story, although they can usually give a clear insight. For example, Muttiah Muralitharan has 92 more Test wickets (800 altogether), nearly twice as many five-fers (67) and 12 more ten-fers (22) than his nearest rival Shane Warne. He bowled in 43 fewer innings than Warne and ended with a better economy, strike rate and average.

But it is universally acknowledged that Warne is the best there's been. Murali was merely a brilliant and consistent spinner, who revelled in the task of carrying his attack.

Yet, the highest wicket stats reveal plenty about the shifting emphasis of cricket through the last 120 years. Only two bowlers who played prior to 1970 ever took more than 300 wickets (Lance Gibbs and Fred Trueman) and those two crept past the landmark.

The first-class game – rather than Test matches – used to carry much more resonance. Murali and Warne's achievements lose some lustre, when you consider that Wilfred Rhodes took more than 4,000 wickets for Yorkshire over 32 seasons, with 67 ten-fers thrown in for good measure. Perhaps even more astonishing, Tich Freeman played almost half as many matches, but snared 3,700 victims, with all of 137 ten-wicket hauls. Both bowlers had their heyday in the 1920s.

Left: England fast bowler Freddie Trueman is applauded by fans as he returns to the Pavilion after taking his 301st Test wicket in the final Ashes match of the 1964 summer at The Oval. He was the first bowler to take 300 Test wickets.

Right: One of cricket's most economical and dangerous fast bowlers, Glenn McGrath celebrating his 500th Test wicket in 2005.

1974

Run Machines

One hypothetical way to identify the leading batsman of each generation is to see who held the record for most Test runs during their playing career.

Things start to get interesting in 1902 when Australia's Clem Hill skips past England's Archie McLaren to post a total of 3,412 runs. Jack Hobbs raises the bar in 1924 to 5,410 (along with nearly 60,000 more runs in first-class cricket), a figure that stays firm until Wally Hammond passes it in 1937.

Greats such as George Headley, Denis Compton, and even Don Bradman himself don't appear on the list. Indeed, Hammond sits tight until 1970, when Colin Cowdrey nips in for a couple of seasons. Gary Sobers finally wrests the title away from England, being the first batsman to reach 8,000 runs in Tests. Geoff Boycott nudges him out by less than a hundred in 1981, but his glory is short lived, as India's Sunil Gavaskar rattles past and continues to over 10,000 runs.

The Aussies post their first champ since Hill, when Allan Border topples Gavaskar and enters the 11,000s. Will Steve Waugh carry on past? No, but Brian Lara does, eventually ending his career just shy of 12,000 runs.

Ricky Ponting, Jacques Kallis and Rahul Dravid all pass 12,000 since Lara, but none of them ever exceed Sachin Tendulkar, who is still steaming away in the lead with more than 15,000 runs.

If Test cricket continues to lag behind the shorter formats, Sachin could own the title for many years to come.

Left: England captain Mike Denness shields India's Sunil Gavaskar from celebrating fans after he had completed his century on the third day of the first Test match at Old Trafford in 1974.

Right: Run machine Sachin Tendulkar reacts after becoming the first batsman in history to score 100 international centuries.

1897

Batting Improvisers

Some batsmen play the same steady shots time and again – their strengths and limitations are renowned so they score through the bowler's inaccuracy or impatience. Then there are the crowd pleasers, forever shifting their mode of attack and adapting their technique to find the gaps.

One of England's most important batsmen was "Ranji", the Indian prince Kumar Shri Ranjitsinhji. A prolific run-getter at the turn of the twentieth century, he introduced a range of new strokes – in particular the late cut and leg glance. It's easy to imagine the bowler's frustration at a batsman waiting until the last moment before bringing the bat down and caressing the ball to the boundary, especially the first time!

The necessity to score quickly in Twenty20 cricket has been the mother of invention. Once a party piece, the reverse sweep is now a conventional weapon – even the switch-hit draws fewer gasps than when Kevin Pietersen swatted two cack-handed sixes in 2008. But the Dilscoop (named after Sri Lankan marvel Tillakaratne Dilshan) has more than pride and wicket at stake. Dilshan ducks at the final moment and flicks the ball – hurtling towards him at over 70mph – over the wicketkeeper for four or six.

Brave, foolish, brilliant … sometimes there's nothing the bowler can do but applaud.

Right: Kumar Shri Ranjitsinhji – or Ranji for short – was a master improviser, whose audacious strokeplay evolved batsmanship.

Far Right: Sri Lanka's Tillakaratne Dilshan 'scoops' the ball for six during the ICC World Twenty20 semi-finals at The Oval. West Indian keeper Dinesh Ramdin can only admire. Dilshan was top run scorer in the 2011 ICC World Cup.

1905

Bowling Improvisers

Yet bowlers can improvise, too. The sight of the best batsman bamboozled by a new delivery lifts the heart of any trundler smashed about the park on a sweltering afternoon. Before long the batting fraternity works out what's going on (or appeals to the ICC for a banning) but for those few matches, series or seasons the bowler fills his boots.

Fast bowlers find some joy in well-disguised changes of pace (the slower ball bouncer has made mugs of several batsman) but spinners have a reputation for improvising. English gentleman Bernard Bosanquet rose to star status in the early 1900s when he invented a delivery that looked like a leg break but turned from off to leg – what we now know as the "googly" or "wrong'un". The Australians had never seen it before and his "bosie" ball enjoyed considerable success when pitched on target.

In the 1990s Pakistani off-spinner Saqlain Mushtaq perfected the "doosra" – the off-spinner's equivalent of the googly, which turns from leg to off. In Urdu, doosra means "the other one" – the code to bowl it from his wicketkeeper. Indeed, there's a school of thought that the great West Indian spinner Sonny Ramadhin was bowling the doosra back in the 1950s but chose not to draw attention to it with a catchy name.

Right: What a wrong-un! Bernard James Tindal Bosanquet of Eton, Oxford University, Middlesex and England, enjoyed success – and notoriety – with his googly at the start of the 20th century.

Far Right: South Africa's Paul Adams bowls a chinaman in the 1996 World Cup. His unorthodox 'frog in a blender' style caused batsmen trouble, until they remembered to watch the ball and not the bowler.

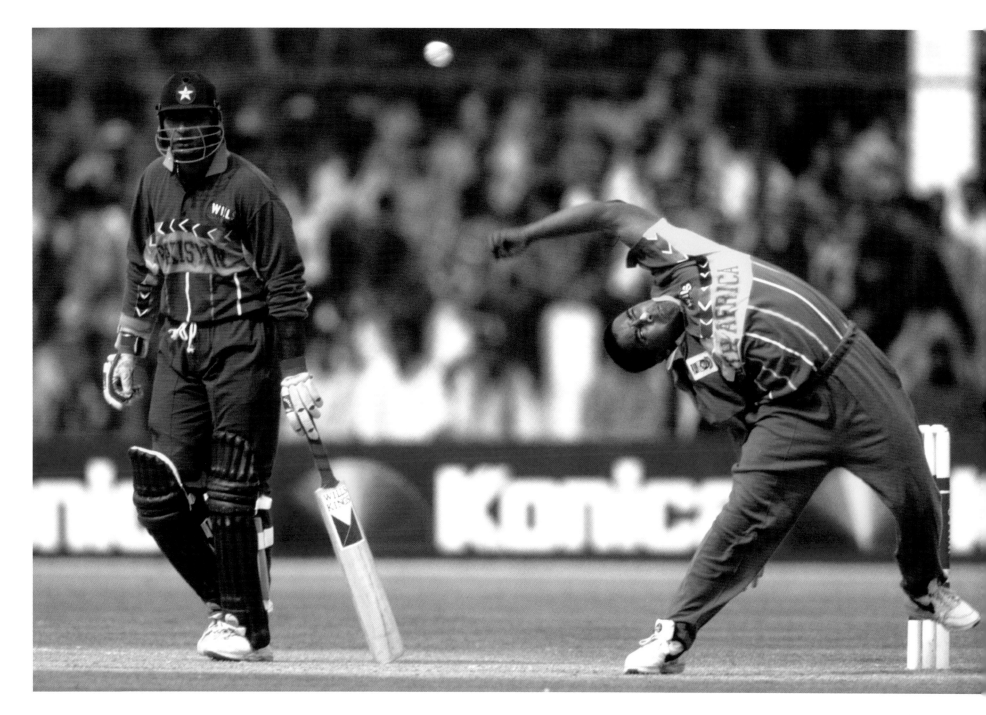

1926

Opening Pairs

Like wine and song, certain opening partnerships prove the perfect match. England's Jack Hobbs and Bert Sutcliffe remain most celebrated of all. With enough talent and concentration to be standouts in their own right, they became more than the sum of their parts from 1924–30.

Hobbs was the senior partner, completely respected by Sutcliffe. The pair enjoyed an almost telepathic understanding, allowing them to run singles with ease for hours on end long before isometric training and ice baths. Even on dog-eared wickets they had to be prised apart.

The stats are remarkable. In 38 innings, they failed to reach 50 for the first wicket on 13 occasions. Their average of 87 runs per innings is 26 runs more than any other at the top of the list. Next come Gordon Greenidge and Desmond Haynes, synonymous with West Indian flair and resolve for more than a decade. They made one more than the 15 century stands of Hobbs and Sutcliffe, albeit in 110 more attempts.

In modern times Australia's Justin Langer and Matthew Hayden often seized the match on the opening day. England's Andrew Strauss and Alastair Cook (11) and India's Virender Sehwag and Gautam Gambhir (10) have yet to chase down the record for most opening centuries.

Left: The crowd look to openers Jack Hobbs (left) and Herbert Sutcliffe to dig England out of a hole, following on during the 1926 Ashes at Headingley. The redoubtable pair constructed a 200-run partnership to save the game.

Right: Justin Langer (left) and Matthew Hayden cross for the winning run at the SCG, sealing an Ashes whitewash in 2007. Langer retired on a high, calling time on the most successful opening double-act in Australian history.

1975

Old Timers

At 42, England's Mark Ramprakash can still cha-cha-cha on the county scene. Yet it's a measure of how much international cricket has changed that India's Rahul Dravid and Sachin Tendulkar were deemed long in the tooth at the age of 39, though both churned out the runs. Playing into one's forties seems odd nowadays, embarrassing even – like the old guy from accounts at the Christmas party, eager for a dance with the intern.

The start of an Indian summer was 40 in yesteryear, however. At the age of 47, the freakish W.G. Grace was first to score 1,000 runs in May (1894) and was still carting first-class bowlers for plenty when he was 54. The indefatigable Yorkshireman Wilfred Rhodes, too, played four Tests against the West Indies as a 52-year-old.

If ever there was a moment to mark the changing of the guard it was the optimistic (naïve?) decision to bring Colin Cowdrey to Australia in 1974–75. Measuring 42 in years and girth, England's erstwhile champion was pitched in against the combined venom of Dennis Lillee and Jeff Thomson. In truth, he fared no worse than others much younger but the clash of pumped-up, long-haired rebels against the portly, albeit polite patrician proved stark. Players since then have been wise not to overstay their welcome for fear of comparison.

Right: Watch your back! David Lloyd looks concerned for 42-year-old Colin Cowdrey as he ducks under a Dennis Lillee heatseeker in 1975.

Far Right: India's Rahul Dravid scrambles back to safety at the WACA in his last Test series against Australia in 2012. He retired soon afterwards, aged 39 – a time of life when W.G. Grace entered his prime.

23

1930

Young Stars

"If you're good enough, you're old enough," as the saying goes. However, it's one that England tends to ignore, waiting until a player has developed his technique (or bad habits) in the county game. On the sub-continent, selectors are more progressive and "Little Master" Sachin Tendulkar clearly owned a talent that needed to flourish on the world stage.

Even the most hard-hearted pragmatist might have felt a pang of sympathy for the tiny, baby-faced 16-year-old with curly hair, who was walking out to bat in Karachi at 41 for 4 against the pace attack of Waqar Younis, Wasim Akram and Imran Khan. Also on debut, Waqar literally blooded Sachin in Test cricket when he hit him in the mouth.

The Tendulkar v. Bradman debate is rendered even more conjectural when one considers there were those who viewed "The Don" as the second best batsman of his generation in the early 1930s.

With a vast array of strokes and lightning footwork, Scottish-born Australian Archie Jackson was hailed the new Victor Trumper. As a 19-year-old in the 1928–29 Ashes series, Jackson scored 164 sumptuous runs on his debut appearance. Sadly this proved to be his peak as his health gradually failed. Tuberculosis finally claimed him at the tender age of 23, robbing cricket of one of its brightest talents.

Right: Could modern medicine have made Australian Archie Jackson – who died of tuberculosis aged 23 – the greatest batsman of all time?

Far Right: Here to stay: a 17-year-old Sachin Tendulkar is applauded by English fielders after scoring his first Test hundred to save the match at Old Trafford in 1990. It wouldn't be his last.

Wicket-keeping

The wicket-keeper's role has greatly changed since the mid-nineteenth century when he was little more than a backstop.

The golden age of keeping arrived in the 1920s and 30s when the catlike Australian Bert Oldfield and hard-hitting Kent man Leslie Ames earned a place in their respective countries' pantheon. Two other Kent keepers stood tall (and crouched low): Godfrey Evans is regarded by those who saw him as the most technically gifted, while Alan Knott was a brilliant wicket-keeper batsman, who would have shone across today's formats. Rodney Marsh was one of Australia's most proficient and popular keepers, taking a hatful of catches – off Dennis Lillee, in particular. In the 1980s, Jamaican Jeff Dujon had the box seat for all those quicks.

During the nineties the keeper's role shifted markedly toward being a run-getter, not saver. England's leading scorer Alec Stewart edged ahead of the gifted Jack Russell before Adam Gilchrist raised the bar still higher in changing the face of batting, let alone wicket-keeping. Current glovesmen Kumar Sangakkara, MS Dhoni, Matt Prior, Brad Haddin and Brendon McCullum could represent their countries on batting ability alone.

Right: West Indian wicket-keeper Sammy Guillen runs out Australia's skipper Lindsay Hassett at the MCG in 1952. Guillen would later qualify for New Zealand and complete that nation's first ever Test victory with a stumping… against the West Indies.

Far Right: Australia's wicket-keeper extraordinaire Adam Gilchrist dives at the WACA in 2008 against India. An outstanding attacking batsman, his all-round skills meant keepers would never again be picked purely for their glovework.

1921

Big Men

Cricket has long enjoyed a reputation for being a sport that may suit the less athletic. After all, if you can catch the ball in the slips and smash it to the boundary often enough why waste time on shuttle runs or low-carb diets? And if someone's gone to the trouble of laying on a fine tea or a slab of lager tinnies, it's rude to say no.

Some of the greatest batsmen to represent their country produced moments of fine athleticism without ever looking like athletes. W.G. Grace himself sported a fine waistline. One of Australia's most successful (and controversial) captains, Warwick "Big Ship" Armstrong was a real bear, apparently weighing in at more than 22 stone, but with enough puff to smack England for three hundreds during the whitewash Ashes of 1920–21. Modern cricketers are expected to be more lissom and agile, scampering quick singles and sliding to save runs in a manner that would have sorely tested the stitches on Big Ship's flannels!

This nostalgia perhaps explains the joy that Bermuda's policeman-come-spinner Dwayne Leverock brought to the 2007 World Cup. In the mismatch pool encounter between the small island and the sub-continent, Bermuda suffered one of the heaviest defeats on record yet still managed to hog the following day's back pages. The reason for this was Leverock's diving catch, launching his 18-stone frame sideways at second slip to snare Robin Uthappa one-handed in the second over. Mighty India were being routed, 3 for 1! So, India didn't lose another wicket for 200 runs and Leverock eventually finished with 1 for 96, but Bermuda won the battle for hearts and minds.

Left: "Big Ship" Warwick Armstrong, Australia's inspirational captain, puts some weight into a drive during his final match against England in 1921. He would only make 19, but he had plenty of other success over the old enemy to reflect on.

Right: Bermudan policeman Dwayne Leverock plods between the wickets during the 2007 World Cup against India, after defying gravity to pull off one of the catches of the tournament.

1946

Brothers In Arms

Back in the early days of Test cricket, the Australian Bannerman and the Gregory brothers starred for their home country. Since then there have been any number of fraternal triumphs, including Flower, Waugh (twins) and Crowe (cousin Russell went into acting instead).

Three blood brothers on the pitch representing their country at the same time is a wee bit special, though. Mrs Grace was apparently a formidable woman but even her heart must have swelled to see her sons play for England in 1880. W.G. was the biggest cheese, but Edward and Fred were good enough to make selection. This proved to be their only Test – Edward was at the end of his career while poor old Fred (who bagged a pair) died of pneumonia a few weeks later.

The Chappells – Ian, Greg and Trevor – all played for Australia in Tests and one-dayers, albeit never simultaneously. Today, Pakistan's Akmal boys – Kamran, Umar and Adnan – share wicket-keeping duties. Top of the brotherly heap, however, is the Mohammad family, four of whom scored hundreds for Pakistan during the 1950s, 60s and 70s. Hanif was most celebrated, but Mushtaq, Wazir and Sadiq were also hugely talented. In 1969, three Mohammads (not Wazir) took the field in a Test against New Zealand to emulate the Graces.

Right: The identical Bedser twins – Eric (padding up) and Alec – were instrumental in Surrey's dominance during the 1950s. Alec emerged as one of England's finest – and gutsiest – bowlers, eventually knighted for services to cricket.

Far Right: Steve and Mark Waugh on the eve of the first Test between Australia and South Africa in 2001. The Test was the 100th the twins had played together.

1905

Split Loyalties

As Test cricket found its feet, it wasn't too far-fetched to find a cricketer swapping from one team to another or even lining up against his sibling in international matches, such were the practicalities of long-distance travel.

Frank Hearne toured South Africa with England in 1889 and enjoyed the climate so much that he stayed behind. The next time England toured he was picked to play for the home side, lining up against his two baby brothers, George and Alec. To make matters even more complicated for the commentators (if there had been any), Jack Hearne (no relation) was also playing for England at the same time.

Albert Trott represented both Australia and England in the Golden Age, something impossible in Test cricket today. And yet England still benefits from players who emigrated from South Africa and Zimbabwe, including Albert's descendant, Jonathan Trott. Recently, Eoin Morgan and Ed Joyce transferred from Ireland's one-day team to the England Test squad. But cricketing history has a habit of repeating itself and Australia have recently blooded James Pattinson, a young fast bowler with a big future. His Test debut comes a few years after his brother Darren was plucked from obscurity to play for England, his birth country. Australia appear to have snaffled the better brother, as Darren played just one Test for England, while James is already building the foundations for a long and glittering career.

Right: Albert Trott – the Albatrott – played for both Australia and England during the Golden Age, and famously smashed a six over the Pavilion at Lord's. A force of nature as a player, he eventually committed suicide, failing to adapt to life after cricket.

Far Right: South African-born Jonathan Trott dives in vain to regain his ground during his debut innings against Australia in the 2009 Ashes at The Oval. He made a century in the second innings to help regain the urn.

1975

Ultimate Turn Offs

Tall, artful and Australian, Hugh Trumble was probably the first great off-spinner, taking 141 wickets in Tests, including two hat-tricks. But for the Golden Age of off-spin, we must look to the 1950s, 60s and 70s when several tweakers emerged as purveyors of skill and stamina.

Hugh Tayfield and Sonny Ramadhin took bundles of wickets during the 1950s before handing the baton to Lance Gibbs and the wizardly Bishan Singh Bedi. Between them, Jim Laker, Fred Titmus and Ray Illingworth gave England control and penetration for 25 years. It's hard to pick the best but Gibbs' 300-plus wickets at less than two runs an over possibly edges it.

Recently, there have been some equally wily and effective offies. Saqlain Mushtaq did not reap the wickets his talents deserved, equally Harbhajan Singh does not always receive the plaudits due his 400 Test wickets, but Graeme Swann's second coming for England has taken player and country to world No. 1. However, none of them come close to Muttiah Muralitharan. For all the controversy and bitterness dogging his career, the Sri Lankan never stopped trying, smiling and taking Test wickets – 800 of them! His effect is immeasurable, an important factor in lifting Sri Lanka from second tier to top table. Whenever "Murali" played, the island had an even or better chance of winning.

Right: Lance Gibbs, famed for his consistency and stamina, gives the ball some flight against the Australians at the MCG in 1975, a match and series the home side dominated.

Far Right: Muttiah Muralitheran bowls his final delivery on home soil, claiming Kiwi Scott Styris leg-before during the 2011 World Cup semi-final.

1930

You Ripper!

Wrist leg spin creates risk and reward for the bowler and for the captain and selectors, too. Inevitably the leg-spinner bowls more half-trackers and full-bungers than your finger-spinning offie and may render the batsman impotent, especially in the fourth innings. However, the potential to cost his skipper runs often sees his place given to an extra-quick/steady off-spinning all-rounder.

The best leggies have been of stout resolve, brimming with self-confidence. While Don Bradman received much of the 1930s and 40s plaudits, he bowled just 20 overs in his Test career and took a solitary wicket. Many of those victories were earned through the uncompromising aggression of Bill "Tiger" O'Reilly and the tireless accuracy of Clarrie Grimmett.

In the 1934 Ashes series in England, the latter strangled the Old Enemy, taking 28 and 25 wickets, respectively. However, both fade beside Shane Warne, arguably, the greatest spin bowler of all. More devastating than his predecessors at their peak, the blond Victorian's effect on the puts him in the highest pantheon.

Warne was mesmerising when he bowled. The batsman was never fully on top, you could not better him for long: that delivery against Mike Gatting, the Ashes' hauls, hundreds of wickets … all impressive but he will surely be remembered for bringing much-needed variety and new mastery to cricket.

Right: Bamboozled, England's Jack Hobbs turns to find he has been clean bowled by the cultured leg spin of Australia's Clarrie Grimmett in 1930.

Far Right: Sixty-three years later, Shane Warne picks up the leg-spinning baton, rocking Mike Gatting's castle with the 'ball of the century' at Old Trafford, his first delivery in the Ashes.

1980

Umpiring Showdowns

Before the days of independent umpires, the touring side often felt they needed to get past 13 members of the opposition. Mostly a shake of the head or a double teapot would register disappointment for a decision at best ill judged. Occasionally gestures became more suggestive, inflammatory even.

In 1980 the mighty West Indies arrived in New Zealand expecting to brush their hosts aside. But Kiwi star performer Richard Hadlee – equally effective on a quick pitch – took 11 wickets. Twelve of the 20 West Indies' wickets were given lbw, seven to Hadlee – a record for the same bowler in a single Test, leading the visitors to claim foul play.

When local umpire John Hastie denied Michael Holding a gloved catch behind, although the keeper took the ball in front of the slips, the seal broke. Holding kicked the stumps down in a show of frustration undermined by the gracefulness of the photo.

There was no such elegance with the finger-wagging showdown between England captain Mike Gatting and Pakistani umpire Shakoor Rana (1987). The trigger was Gatting's field change as the bowler ran in and demonstrated the ill feeling following a series of repeated gaffs. Forced to apologise, Gatting was swiftly axed while Rana became a national hero.

Cricket finally cottoned on that impartial umpires were a priority.

Left: Michael Holding's patience runs out when the latest in a series of umpiring decisions goes against him in Dunedin in 1980. Showing superb goal-kicking form, Holding smashed down the stumps after a clear catch was turned down.

Right: England captain Mike Gatting seethes as he walks away from Pakistan umpire Shakoor Rana. The pair clashed following a number of controversial incidents throughout the 1987 series.

1967

Rabbits in the Headlights

Tail-enders can be a source of great crowd amusement, but the arrival of certain number elevens down the years has heralded a virtual stampede to the refreshment tents. Everybody, including the batsman himself, knows this will be mercifully short: one full, straight, quick-ish ball probably suffices. And if the "walking wicket" is not out immediately, his pal at the other end will most likely perish trying to smash some bonus runs before the inevitable occurs.

The original forlorn hope was Australian Jack Saunders, an impressive left-arm spinner and an integral part of the 1902 Ashes win in England. In his career he took 79 wickets at just 22 runs apiece and could be unplayable on a wet pitch, but he was a terrible batsman. Only once in 23 innings did he reach double figures, scoring 39 runs – half his wickets – at an average of 2.29.

New Zealand's Chris Martin is often credited as the world's worst batsman. With 109 runs from 90 innings (202 wickets taken to date), he makes a good case. Statistically at least, he has a better batting average than Zimbabwean Pommie Mbangwa, who retired into television commentary with an even two runs per dismissal. That Mbangwa managed more runs (34) than wickets (32) perhaps says more about his bowling ability…

Right: Indian spinner Bhagwat Chrandresekhar fails again in 1967 on tour in England. A withered right hand, which never hampered his bowling, made gripping the bat difficult and he rarely lasted long at the crease.

Far Right: Chris Martin has collected many more wickets than runs in his Test career. When he walks to the middle, the ground staff fire up the roller.

1966

All Round Brilliance

So, who were cricket's greatest all-rounders? That slightly depends on your definition. W.G. Grace (hurdles, crown green bowls), C.B. Fry (long jump, football, classicist), Denis Compton (football), Sir Conrad Hunte (human rights supporter), Richie Benaud (iconic broadcaster) and Imran Khan (politics) all achieved greatness beyond the field of play.

On the pitch, if we go with the premise that a genuine all-rounder allows his team to enter the match with a virtual twelfth man, certain names stand out. The incomparable S.F. Barnes could spin or swing the ball at will. With the recent emphasis on wicketkeeper-batsmen, glovemen like Adam Gilchrist, Alec Stewart, M.S. Dhoni and Kumar Sangakkara number among the finest-ever blades.

Freddie Flintoff, Shane Watson, Dwayne Bravo, Daniel Vettori and Shakib Al Hasan repeatedly made their mark in the last decade, but of the modern players only South Africa's prolific Jacques Kallis rivals the eighties quartet of Ian Botham, Imran Khan Richard Hadlee and Kapil Dev. Top of the tree must still be Barbadian Garry Sobers. For both style and substance, his batting was unforgettable – even without the 365 not out and six sixes. Sobers could bowl quickly with the new ball, finger and wrist spin with the old; field in any position. He could probably have made it as a golfer or basketball player, too. A leader, an ambassador, an inspiration, he is the perfect all-rounder.

Left: Sir Garfield Sobers, the most complete cricketer of all time, bowls at Arundel for the West Indies. He was like four players rolled into one, brilliant at fielding, batting, pace bowling and spin.

Right: Underrated colossus Jacques Kallis of South Africa hits out against England at Headingley in 2003. Statistically, at least, he's the best all-rounder ever to play the game.

1938

Head Hunters

Until the 1970s the best fast bowlers used their bouncer sparingly. Persistent short-pitched bowling could be effective but the batsmen were soon be set and the bowler tired. But slip in the occasional effort ball, spitting at the chest from just back of a length, and the batsman must glove it or wear it.

Those skilful enough to drag the batsman forward in previous overs are the most dangerous headhunters. Seeing the batsman arched like a leaping salmon as he throws his body out of the path of a 90+ mph heat-seeker is a real treat. Genuine quicks, like Ray Lindwall, Frank Tyson, Michael Holding, Jeff Thomson, Alan Donald, Brett Lee and Shoaib Akhtar, could hurry the best through raw pace while the height of Joel Garner, Curtly Ambrose, Glenn McGrath and Steve Harmison found bounce where others struggled. Malcolm Marshall and Wasim Akram were apparently most scary for the ball would skid up at alarming speed – no escape!

Once the fast bowling community smells blood or indeed the selectors sense a weakness against short-pitched bowling, a Test batsman's career quickly folds. Australia's Michael Bevan (who averaged more than 53 in one-dayers) was deemed flaky against the short stuff and never really made it in Tests. Today's Phil Hughes and Suresh Raina are trying to prove they have the right nerve and technique. Luckily, there are no Marshalls or Akrams out there.

Left: Sussex's Jim Cornford takes off in his effort to ping the ball at the batsman in a County Championship match against Essex in 1938. The opening bowler was a stalwart for Sussex for 20 years, taking more than 1,000 first-class wickets.

Right: England batsman Hugh Morris takes evasive action against West Indian speedster Patrick Patterson – one of the most fearsome bowlers of all time – during a Test at Edgbaston in 1991. Even the unshakeable Graham Gooch admitted to being frightened by Patterson.

1980

Scoring Fast

Despite ever quickening scoring rates, a hundred before lunch remains a notable event. It has only ever happened 20 times in Test matches, with just four hundreds on the first morning. The first three were in England by Australian kingpins Victor Trumper, Charlie McCartney (dropped in the first over) and Don Bradman. Only Pakistani Majid Khan has managed one since (against New Zealand, 1976).

For speed of scoring, there have been some notable destroyers. Gilbert Jessop (1902) set the target, smashing a hundred in 77 balls in an hour and a quarter. From the belly of defeat, he snatched victory, playing one of the finest-ever Ashes innings. Viv Richards, naturally, holds the record for all-time fastest – 56 deliveries against England at his Antigua home ground in 1986. Intriguingly, the next fastest by a West Indian is not Chris Gayle, Brian Lara nor Gordon Greenidge, but limpet Shivnarine Chanderpaul who unleashed an even hundred in 69 balls v. Australia in 2003.

With the advent of "pinch-hitting" in one-day internationals, Test run-rates escalated. ODI openers Adam Gilchrist, Sanath Jayasuriya, Virender Sehwag and Gayle, among others, transferred skills to the Test arena, while the dominant Aussies simply got on with it. Doubtless David Warner – a T20 generation product – will go faster than his recent 69-ball ton against India and may even threaten Viv's benchmark.

Left: Pakistani batsman Majid Khan, one of just four batsmen ever to score a hundred before lunch on the first day of a Test, lofts one into the leg side against the West Indies in 1980.

Right: Demolition Derby: Australia's David Warner spanks another six off the Indian bowlers at the WACA during his 69-ball ton.

1927

Lady Cricketers

There are records of competitive women's cricket dating back as far as 1745 – "eleven maids of Bramley and eleven maids of Hambleton, dressed all in white," according to the *Reading Mercury*. For the next two centuries, though, the female public persona of cricket revealed itself in exhibition matches, often attended in their thousands, with the spectators drawn to the opportunities for courting, leering and gambling as much as the play itself.

Behind the scenes, women also played their part in the development of men's cricket. John Willes, who is credited with introducing round-armed bowling at the start of the nineteenth century, apparently learned the art from his sister Christina, who could not bowl underarm due to her billowing skirts. And would W.G. Grace have been quite the force without his deeply knowledgeable and ambitious mother, Martha?

The first women's Test (between England and Australia) was not until 1934, when a talented squad of English ladies, including the brilliant Molly Hide, toured for six months unbeaten. Since then the game has grown, especially in the 1960s and 70s, under the direction of England's Rachael Heyhoe-Flint, who led her nation to victory in the first World Cup (1973) – a feat the men have yet to emulate. Under Charlotte Edwards, England claimed the latest trophy in 2009.

Left: Dolly drops: a 1920's belle lobs the ball towards the batswoman from deep within the crease, no doubt bringing her midwicket and mid-on into play.

Right: Pace and poise: quick bowler Ellyse Perry of the Australian Southern Stars sends one down during a Twenty20 match against New Zealand at the North Sydney Oval in 2012.

Left: William Gilbert Grace, arguably cricket's most important player for his role in establishing its popularity. Such was his fame and national standing, he rubbed shoulders with the future King of England.

Right: Fans, both young and old, cheer on Sachin Tendulkar against the West Indies in his home town of Mumbai in 2011. Sachin fell just short of his 100th international hundred, in a match that ended as a draw with the scores level.

1905

Influence Beyond the Game

Measuring a cricketer's importance is much trickier than gauging his relative ability as the focus widens far beyond the boundary ropes. Don Bradman, for example, was a peerless batsman, but also played an invaluable role in bolstering Australian spirits during the Depression. Jack Hobbs provided light relief after the First World War, Denis Compton after the Second. Sir Viv Richards – a defiant figurehead who brought equality, then dominance for the West Indies – lit fires in Babylon.

When it comes to fame and influence, however, two names stand out. W.G. Grace's effect in the second half of the nineteenth century is arguably unmatched in any other sport; his accomplishments on wretched pitches unparalleled among peers. Such was his popularity (and notoriety) that cricket evolved from a hobby game into a professional sport that dominated the English summer and spread worldwide. We're still benefiting from this force of nature.

Sachin Tendulkar never sought the limelight, but has filled it magnificently for more than two decades, carrying the hopes and ambitions of millions in his homeland and abroad. With such early fame and fortune, he might be forgiven several years off the rails and the occasional scandal, but his quiet integrity has proved vital for the upkeep of cricket's code of conduct. With luck, the next generation will learn from his example.

Two
The Game

The West Indian team celebrates as Australia's Ian Meckiff is run out by a Joe Solomon direct hit in the first Test match at Brisbane during the 1960–61 series. His dismissal resulted in the first tie in Test history.

1930

Big Hundreds

Charles Bannerman began the hunt for big hundreds in the very first Test in 1877, scoring 165 not out; fellow Aussie Billy Murdoch made the first double hundred, seven years later. But it was not until 1930 that England's Andy Sandham made the first triple – against the West Indies in Kingston.

King of "going on" Bradman recorded 12 doubles (including 299 not out) and two triples, although his top score of 334 against England was twice bettered in the 1930s as Englishmen Wally Hammond (336 not out against New Zealand) and Len Hutton (364 against Australia) plundered more.

Hutton's record stood proud until Sir Garfield Sobers overhauled it by a single run (365 not out, 1958) against Pakistan, his maiden Test century. Others nibbled at Sobers' mark – Graham Gooch, for example, was out for 333 against India in 1990. Eventually Brian Lara swallowed it whole in 1994, smashing England for 375. Australia's Matthew Hayden nipped in with 380 against a hapless Zimbabwean attack in 2003, rousing Lara to set the record straight with 400 not out against England the following year.

Only Bradman, Lara, Chris Gayle and Virender Sehwag have twice passed 300, while Pakistani Hanif Mohammed's epic 334 to save a Test in Barbados in 1958 is the only to come in the second innings. Neither a New Zealander nor a South African has reached 300.

Left: Australian folk hero Don Bradman salutes the crowd during his battling innings of 232 at The Oval in 1930, which helped seal the Ashes. In total, he scored 974 runs with four hundreds (two doubles) during the series, a record that still stands.

Right: West Indies captain Brian Lara celebrates reaching 300 at Antigua against England in 2004. He would add another hundred runs to post the highest score in Tests of all time.

1948

Famous Ducks

The most legendary duck in cricketing history needs little introduction. Still a batting phenomenon, Don Bradman (a statistical anomaly in any sport, given the distance between himself and the next best) needed just four runs in his final Test innings to maintain an average above three figures. Walking out to a standing ovation at The Oval, he was at the peak of his powers after another record-breaking tour. With his Test average standing at 101.39, Bradman was four runs shy of 7,000 Test runs. It was written in the stars …

Yet cricket cares not for reputations. Nor, as it happened, did England's leg-spinner Eric Hollies. Bradman negotiated the first ball, but did not pick the googly that followed, which spun back in to rock his castle. W.G. Grace might have held his ground, but Bradman was forced to trudge back to the pavilion as the crowd rose once more.

India's Sourav Ganguly may have ended his career with a batting average less than half of Bradman's but he was a fine blade by normal standards and as a captain cherished by many for transporting their country from mediocrity to leading power. Around Nagpur the hush was deafening as the hero chipped his last ball in Test cricket back to the bowler, who turned his swansong into an unseemly quack.

Right: Don Bradman is bowled for a duck by a googly from Eric Hollies during Australia's second innings in the final Test match against England at The Oval in 1948.

Far Right: India's Sourav Ganguly goes for a golden duck in his last innings during the fourth Test match between India and Australia in 2008.

1952

Collapses

A relaxed dressing room soon descends into a flurry of panicked activity, as the fielding side smells blood. Even the best sides submit to the inexorable slide.

In 1902, Australia arrived in England with one of its finest ever batting attacks. Yet, in the first Test at Edgbaston, these starlets staged Australia's worst ever collapse, all out for 36. In their defence, the pitch was all but unplayable. Without the brilliant Victor Trumper, who battled to 18 runs, they would have set a sorrier benchmark.

The next time Australia came close to breaking that unenviable record, over a century later, there could be no such excuse. In the sunnier climes of Cape Town, Australia's finest – including Hussey, Ponting and Clarke – contrived to be all out for 47, nipped out in just 18 overs by a South African attack with their tails up.

In the circumstances, the last wicket stand of 26 between numbers nine Peter Siddle (12) and eleven Nathan Lyon (14) was a heroic effort, given they joined with the score at 21 for 9. It was just the eighth time in the history of Tests that the last man was top scorer in the innings.

And it showed that some things in cricket never change. When the collapse is on, even the best line-ups crumple like a paper cup in a rainstorm.

Right: The Headingley scoreboard tells the story of an astonishing collapse by India's batsmen at the start of their second innings. In the space of just 14 balls, England claimed four wickets to leave the tourists with 4 wickets down for no runs scored in 1952. England won by 7 wickets.

Far Right: Fall guys: Members of the England cricket team look dejected after being blown away for 46 by Curtly Ambrose to lose a match they could have won in Trinidad in 1994.

1929

Partnerships

It's bad enough watching one batsman cart you about the park all day, but two simultaneously means the fielding side undergoes a gruelling test of morale. A long-lasting partnership proves greatly satisfying for the batsmen, though. English technician Herbert Sutcliffe is renowned for his first wicket stands with Jack Hobbs and fêted in Yorkshire alongside opening county partner Percy Holmes.

The two had formed the bedrock of a decade of White Rose dominance but, by 1932, were getting long in the tooth. Indeed, Holmes was approaching his 45th birthday. On the first day of a County Championship, they showed no signs of fatigue, smashing Essex for a crippling 423 for no loss. On day two, Holmes and Sutcliffe set a new record for a first-class opening stand – 555 – before Sutcliffe was out. Beleaguered Essex inevitably lost by an innings: going down 20 wickets for 242 runs.

In the Test arena the modern era has witnessed some of the meatiest partnerships ever, including a staggering 624 runs between Mahela Jayawardene and Kumar Sangakkara of Sri Lanka against South Africa in 2006. The pair made the most of their right-/left-hand differences, milking spinner Nicky Boje for 221 runs from 65 wicketless overs. Failure to seize a wicket for two sessions is tough enough; extend that to two days in blazing Colombo sunshine and the fielding side is on its knees.

Left: English cricketing icons Jack Hobbs and Herbert Sutcliffe come out to bat in Australia in 1929. Wally Hammond stole the headlines, but the two openers both averaged over 50 in a series dominated by the visitors.

Right: Sri Lankan master craftsmen Kumar Sangakkara (right) and Mahela Jayawardene take stock of their astonishing partnership against South Africa in Colombo in 2006. Note the figures of Nicky Boje…

Limpets

In certain series the bowler can become so accustomed to seeing a batsman in the middle that he almost feels part of their own team. Whatever the bowler does, he is unable to prise his rival out cheaply, leading to a kind of resignation that the batsman is there to stay. Once this occurs, the bowler forgets about him altogether to concentrate on the others.

Legendary batsman Everton Weekes set the benchmark for total dominance over an opposition in a single series as he laid waste to India in 1948. Fresh from a 100 against England, he scored four consecutive 100s in India, followed by two more 50s for good measure. His back-to-back five tons remains a record that he would almost certainly have extended, if not for a dodgy run-out decision on 90.

Weekes' West Indian heir apparent has been the Guyanan Shivnarine Chanderpaul, who continues to churn out run after run while those about him surrender their wicket with barely a whimper. In Tests, only six batsmen have ever batted for more than 1,000 minutes (over 16 hours) in consecutive innings without being dismissed. "Shiv" has done so a staggering four times. In 2006–07, batting in the varying conditions of Pakistan, England and South Africa, the quirky left-hander finally matched Weekes' achievement of seven 50s in a row.

Left: Statement of intent: a young Geoff Boycott dead bats a ball from Garth McKenzie during his debut innings in the 1964 Ashes Test at Trent Bridge. Boycott made 48, but missed the second innings in the draw after a fielding injury.

Right: 'The Wall' Rahul Dravid digs one out at Lord's during one of three defiant hundreds in 2011, as England secured a 4-0 whitewash.

1985

Bad Run of Form

Anyone bottling and selling confidence to sportsmen would make a mint. For talented batsman Mohinder "Jimmy" Amarnath, self-belief was high in the early eighties. Aside from helping India win the 1983 World Cup, he scored heaps in extremis against Pakistan and the West Indies on the road. When the latter visited India in 1983, the right-hander was his side's big hope. To say he bombed is an understatement – a pair in the first Test seemed to drain confidence from him, his legs became jelly. One and then zero in the next saw him sidelined for the following two. A fifth-Test return yielded another pair. One run in six innings earned him the moniker "Amarnought".

Bad times encourage us to gorge later, which perhaps explains England captain Andrew Strauss's hunger for Test runs and Series victories. His career started brightly – hundreds galore and stirring wins against South Africa, then Australia in 2005. Passed over for the captaincy, the runs dried up. Edges flew to hand, decisions went against him and with barely a 50 in 20 innings, Strauss entered selectorial last chance saloon during a series in New Zealand in 2008. After several more low scores, his race looked run. But in the second innings of the final Test, 177 saved his career, secured the series – and England have been winning Tests ever since.

Right: Neil Foster celebrates the key wicket of Mohinder Amarnath in Chennai. Foster got him twice in that 1985 Test, although Amarnath made 78 and 95. Two years earlier, Amarnath managed just one run in six innings against the West Indies.

Far Right: Andrew Strauss leaves the field with just two runs to his name at Hamilton in 2008, as England slumped to defeat. He made a big hundred two Tests later at Napier to secure the series and put his career back on track.

1971

Catches Win Matches

Anywhere in the world you play cricket, from Cootamundra to Chelmsford, Cape Town to Chennai, at some point during the day you will hear the following: "Come on, lads, catches win matches!" because it's true – and especially so in a tight-run chase.

In 1982, at the MCG, Allan Border and last-man Jeff Thomson came within a whisker of winning a Test match that looked far beyond them, somehow reducing the target on the last day from 74 to four. Just as England's world was caving in, Ian Botham served up a juicy long hop, which Thomson guided into the slips. Chris Tavaré palmed it in the air, but then second slip Geoff Miller somehow grabbed the rebound, denying Australia a famous victory.

The Aussies went on to win that Series, but in 2005 Geraint Jones' tumbling catch to dismiss Michael Kasprowicz at Edgbaston in the second Test was the moment England realised they could regain the Ashes after a generation's wait. It wasn't the trickiest keeper's catch, looping up off the gloves from a well-aimed Steve Harmison bouncer, but had he slipped or snatched at the ball, there would have been no victory parade, no biographies, no MBEs. In terms of happiness for English supporters and financial benefit for English players, has there ever been a more important catch?

Left: Close fielder Eknath Solkar takes a crucial diving catch to dismiss Alan Knott at The Oval in 1971, as England subsided for just 101. India eventually won the nail-biter, securing their first Test series victory in England.

Right: Last gasp: Geraint Jones eyeballs the catch that levelled the 2005 Ashes at Edgbaston, securing the nerve-shredder by two runs. Had he grassed it, there probably would have been no way back in the series.

1966

Butterfingers!

Catches may well win matches, yet in cricketers' all-too-often pessimistic outlook, it is the dropped catches that linger longest in the memory.

Perhaps the most costly in terms of a Test match came in 1936, when England were 2-0 up in the five-match series against Don Bradman's Australians at the MCG. England were ahead in the match, just a few wickets away from another easy victory and regaining the Ashes. When Bradman came to the crease in the second innings, fast bowler Bill Voce brought a false shot from the great man's first ball, which headed straight down Walter Robins' throat at deep square leg.

"Oh, don't give it another thought, Walter," pronounced captain Gubby Allen, as the ball lay on the turf. "You've just cost us the Ashes, that's all." Indeed he had. Bradman scored 270, won the match, then pummelled England for the next two to retain the coveted urn.

For sheer volume of runs lost, though, poor old Chris Scott of Durham made his mark in cricketing history in 1994, playing against Warwickshire. The wicketkeeper dropped a routine edge from Brian Lara, then in the form of his life, on just 18. "I suppose he'll get a hundred now," said Scott. Lara made 501 not out, the highest knock in first-class cricket... Whoopsy!

Right: West Indian Seymour Nurse dives forward in a vain attempt to catch Tom Graveney at Lord's in 1966. Graveney made 94 in the first innings and 30 not out in the second to help bat out the draw.

Far Right: England spinner Graeme Swann can't hide his frustration as his captain Andrew Strauss drops West Indian batsman Shivnarine Chanderpaul in Barbados in 2009. Swann took a five-fer, but the West Indies eventually declared for 749!

1970

Six!

It may yield just two more runs than a four edged through the slips but a booming six smashed over the boundary into the stands carries far greater weight for the batting side. Due to better bats, shorter boundaries, flatter pitches, stronger and fitter batsmen and T20, sixes are much more common in the modern game.

But this is not such a new phenomenon. After all, in the early 1900s Gilbert Laird Jessop (known as "Croucher" for his unorthodox stance) could flay the bowlers, should the mood take him. His famous battering of Australia at The Oval turned the match with a hundred in just 75 minutes, with five big sixes and 17 fours on a dodgy track using the sort of bat you might see on pub walls.

And the most famous six ever struck? Well, it's hard to say. Sir Gary Sobers' sixth of six in the over of 1968 off quiz-favourite Malcolm Nash is certainly up there. Pakistani legend Javed Miandad deserves a mention, too, launching India's Chetan Sharma into the stands with a boundary needed to win, so lifting the Austral-Asia Cup in 1986. But for pure theatre, captain Mahendra Singh Dhoni's massive maximum to clinch the 2011 World Cup in front of his adoring Indian fans must be the most iconic to date.

Left: Clive Lloyd, batting for the Rest of the World against England at Trent Bridge in 1970, pulls the ball over the backward square leg boundary for six.

Right: Demonstrating how to win in style. Mahendra Singh Dhoni uppercuts a six in front of a passionate home crowd during the 2011 ICC World Cup Final between India and Sri Lanka.

1905

One-Test Wonders

Spare a thought for those unfortunate cricketers who were clearly talented yet failed to step up to Test standard when opportunity knocked. The original one-Test flop was Fred Tate, all the way back in 1902. Having taken 180 wickets in the summer, Fred's form as a bowler was not in question. Indeed the Ashes series was on a knife-edge when Tate was brought in to bolster the bowling.

Alas, he suffered a horror debut on the first day, bowling too short and beckoning Victor Trumper to smack a hundred before lunch. In the field he dropped a dolly, crucially switching the momentum back to Australia. And he was last man out, with England needing just three runs to win. The Ashes were lost and Tate never played for his country again. He did at least take a couple of wickets and a catch in that match … and went on to father Maurice Tate, one of England's finest bowling all-rounders.

In 1999 poor old Gavin Hamilton failed to contribute a solitary run, catch or wicket in his sole outing for England as the South Africans dismantled the touring side at the Wanderers. At the peak of his profession, he was found lacking.

'Tis better to have played and lost than never to have played at all, though.

Right: Frederick William Tate endured a torrid debut, losing the match with both ball and bat. The match was named after him and he would never play again for England.

Far Right: After a long wait as a county pro, Alan Wells was picked for England, only to nick one off Curtly Ambrose first ball at The Oval in 1995. He made three not out, from 39 balls, in the second innings to secure the draw, and that was his lot.

1960

Even Stevens

While some "bore draws" or one-sided contests try the patience of the most diehard, a tie can produce high drama. In such tense finishes the run-out takes centre stage while desperate batsmen attempt lunatic singles.

The first tie in Tests unfolded at Brisbane in 1960. The West Indies got a century from Gary Sobers but a ton from Norm O'Neill and ten wickets from Alan Davidson put Australia on top. As the match reached its climax, Australia were seven runs short of victory with two overs remaining and four wickets in hand. Davidson was on 80 with captain Richie Benaud well set on 52. But he called Davidson through for a dodgy single and could only curse his flagrancy when Joe Solomon threw down the stumps.

After Benaud was himself out to a hook shot, the Windies' fielders, sensing panic, closed in on nine, ten, Jack. Wicketkeeper Wally Grout and number 10 Ian Meckiff edged the total down to three needed off three balls: one hit would do it. Grout hit the ball to the midwicket boundary, ran the first two hard and attempted the third, but was run out by a bullet throw from Conrad Hunte. Scores level. One wicket left.

With everyone round the bat, No. 11 Lindsay Kline knew he must tip and run. But Meckiff could not beat the throw from Solomon, who hit with one stump to aim at. Match tied.

Right: Australia's tailenders hold on for a draw in the closely-fought 1960–61 series against the West Indies at Adelaide, a series that featured the first tied match.

Far Right: Last pair Graham Onions and Graeme Swann of England celebrate a plucky draw off the last ball against South Africa at Newlands in 2010. Wicketkeeper Mark Boucher voices his frustration.

1930

Bumper Series

A vital characteristic of the successful batsman is greed. When the stars align, every catch is dropped, the ball always finds the gap, umpiring decisions go your way – you must gorge on runs. "Fill your boots!" cry your bowlers from the pavilion balcony. Feast until the opposition is sick of you, for who knows when the next famine will arrive.

The top batsmen have all had their purple patches. Don Bradman rightly tops the pile for most runs in a single series: 974 in just seven innings against England in the 1930 Ashes. West Indian tyros, including Everton Weekes, Clyde Walcott, Gary Sobers, Viv Richards and Brian Lara, also stand out as relentless gatherers.

In the 2010 Ashes series in Australia, opening batsman Alastair Cook drew comparison with the great Wally Hammond, amassing 766 runs as England romped to a 3-1 victory. Fearsome powers of concentration plus a simplified technique and occasional good fortune kept him at the crease for a total of 36 hours during seven tortuous innings for the Aussie bowlers.

Eighty years previously, albeit in two more innings, Hammond went further: plundering 905 runs, including four hundreds, to secure a thumping 4-1 victory. Two years earlier, a mystery fever had threatened to rob the game of one of its brightest stars and now he was determined to celebrate a return to form.

Right: The Don leaves the Headingley pitch after his rapid 334 (over 300 on the first day) in 1930. He scored just under a thousand runs in only seven innings as Australia regained the Ashes, thereby earning lifelong adoration back home.

Far Right: England's Alastair Cook acknowledges applause for his second hundred in two matches at Adelaide during the 2010 Ashes. He would make another at Sydney, compiling 766 runs in the series, the most for an Englishman since Wally Hammond.

1956

10 Out of 10

Circumstances count when judging the finest performances of all time. On the loose proviso that the world record (400 not out by Brian Lara against England, 2004) is the best a batsman can achieve in a single innings, what works for bowlers? Surely it must be to return the best figures of all time.

Since 1956, 10 out of 10 wickets has been the benchmark when the accurate off-spinner English Jim Laker snared all the Australians for just 53 runs. Everything went his way – the state of the pitch, fallibility of the opposition but most importantly, the inability of spin twin Tony Lock to take a wicket. Lock bowled almost as well as Laker though without a shred of luck. In a performance surely never be repeated, let alone bettered, Laker took 19 wickets in the match. Earlier in that magical summer, the Surrey man also bowled out all 10 Aussies in a first-class warm-up match.

Eventually, in 1999, India's powerhouse Anil Kumble revealed immense stores of resolve and skill in matching Laker's wondrousness. Against a formidable Pakistani line-up, the leg spinner took all 10 for 74 runs in a low-scoring Delhi thriller. A young Harbhajan Singh played the role of Lock, wheeling away for no reward.

Kumble is listed behind Laker, but whose was the better effort?

Left: English bowler Jim Laker (left) is presented with the two balls with which he took 9 and 10 wickets during the Test match at Old Trafford in 1956.

Right: Indian spinner Anil Kumble (right), who took all ten Pakistani wickets in Delhi, 1999, receives a gift from Minister L.K. Adwani in recognition of the feat.

1978

Best Foot Forward

As the ball spears toward him at warp speed, the unsure or nervous batsman's feet will glue to the ground. "Should have got forward," tuts the commentator during the long walk back. One batsman rarely to have taken a backward step, whether with bat or microphone in hand, is Geoffrey Boycott. Such was the Yorkshireman's determination to protect his wicket and make as many runs as possible, personal safety was a side issue. Technically precise, he would come forward against the fastest the West Indies and Australia had to offer, showing the full face of his bat and picking up thousands of runs in the process.

In recent years, Ricky Ponting and Rahul Dravid have shown exemplary front footwork. Michael Vaughan's cover drive marked the start of summer such was its refreshing beauty, while Kevin Pietersen in his pomp works the ball in whatever direction he chooses.

But has any batsman scored more runs off the front foot than Jacques Kallis? Like Boycott, Kallis has been accused of batting too slowly – selfishly, even – but that's to ignore his astonishing record. Even without his haul of 543 wickets and 298 catches in all international cricket, the South African star currently has 40 Test tons, 12,000+ runs and a Test average over 56 – mostly amassed by putting his best foot forward.

Left: Geoff Boycott watches the ball race to the boundary in Karachi, during the third Test against Pakistan in 1978. Boycs scored a half century in the second innings, as England drew in his first match as skipper.

Right: Also at Karachi, this time in 2000, England captain Nasser Hussain hammers the ball as the shadows lengthen on the second day. Hussain was there at the end, as England secured the match and the series in near darkness.

1932

Courage Under Fire

Facing down the finest quicks of his era is an accomplishment every batsman wants to add to his CV. Australian Stan McCabe was seemingly brave as a mongoose during the 1930s, especially against Harold Larwood throughout the Bodyline series when he cut, hooked and pulled the ball off his nose on the way to 187 in Sydney, wearing just the baggy green on his head.

Dennis Amiss' double hundred against the West Indies at The Oval in 1976, when Michael Holding bowled like the wind to take 14 wickets, was by all accounts a veritable masterclass. Likewise, Allan Lamb relished any pace on offer, scoring six hundreds against the West Indian barrage of the 1980s. Kim Hughes' gutsy unbeaten hundred against Holding, Roberts, Garner and Croft of 1981 on a dodgy MCG track marked his greatest hour as Australia edged a low-scoring Test.

Of the modern batsmen Michael Atherton withstood several onslaughts for the English cause, especially against an infuriated Allan Donald. And Ricky Ponting won't stay pegged back for long before counter-punching. But for mastery of the short ball, surely the West Indians lead the charge? Bang it in against Headley, the three Ws, Sobers, Kanhai, Richards, Lara and the rest – and you might get them … occasionally. More likely, you'll go the distance.

Left: Harold Larwood bowls to Stan McCabe during the controversial Bodyline series of 1932–33. McCabe scored a defiant 187 not out in the first Test at Sydney, repeatedly risking injury to hook Larwood from in front of his nose.

Right: Ricky Ponting pulls a short ball from England's Simon Jones on the first day of the 2002–03 Ashes at the Gabba. Ponting made 123 runs, while Jones ruptured an anterior cruciate ligament fielding in the deep.

1980

Stumpings

In Tests, certainly, stumpings have decreased with the advent of covered pitches. When batsmen needed to move their feet more, venturing out of the crease to negate indifferent bounce, they were more in danger of being caught out, and stumped. The most prolific stumper was Aussie Bert Oldfield, claiming 52 in just 54 Tests against 72 catches. In comparison, Adam Gilchrist managed just 37 stumpings against 379 catches, even with Shane Warne bamboozling batsmen. Either Oldfield was a genius or the game has changed.

The most Oldfield managed in an innings was four (against England, 1925), including Jack Hobbs. Then, in 1988, Indian gloveman Kiran More managed five in the second innings against the all-conquering West Indians. On a Chennai "burner", debutant leg-spinner Narendra Hirwani turned the ball square from day one, taking 16 wickets as the Windies flailed in vain at his offerings. Apparently, More did well to hold onto the chances.

In one-day cricket (especially T20), the keeper's ability to stand up to medium pacers – even the quicks – is again an asset. The merit was made clear by eccentric stumper Jack Russell, who won a string of county trophies for Gloucestershire by forcing the batsmen to stay in their crease against medium-paced bowlers. Dictate terms to a batsman and sooner or later, he'll be on his way.

Left: David Bairstow – father of current England hopeful Jonathan – celebrates his stumping of Graeme Wood during the Centenary Test match at Lord's in 1980, although Wood had already made 112.

Right: Look back in anger: Hansie Cronje is stumped by Australian gloveman Ian Healy at The Gabba in Brisbane in 1994.

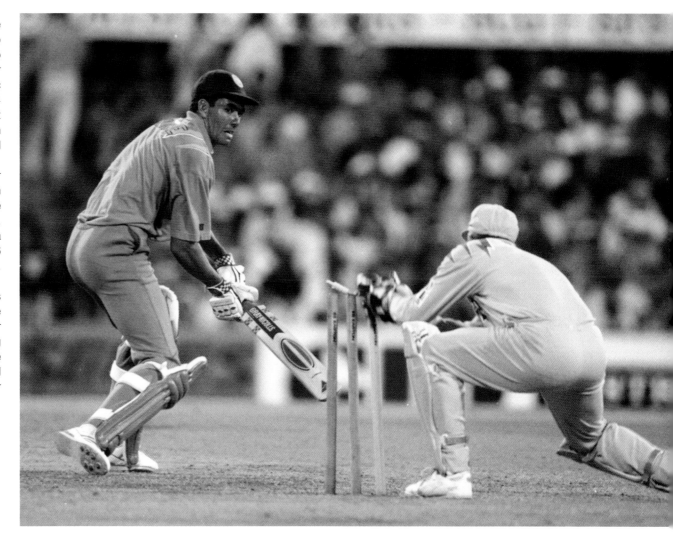

1964

Slip Catches

No surprise many fine slip fielders are also masterful batsmen – just as the ace batsman seems to have more time, so the expert fielder sees the ball into his hands in slow motion. Supreme catcher Wally Hammond was best of his generation – apparently never needing to dive, such was his anticipation and speed. Australia's proud history in the cordon is led by Bobby Simpson, who can lay claim to being the only non-keeper to come close to a catch per innings average (110 in 117 innings). Greg Chappell, Allan Border, Mark Taylor, Shane Warne, Ricky Ponting – all amazing – but the best by popular opinion was Mark Waugh, who made the sublime appear everyday.

Ian Botham and Viv Richards were superb – edge the ball against Somerset and you were on your way. Botham would stand forward of his peers at second slip, backing himself to take half-chances, while Viv was often accompanied by four or five others in a cordon of doom.

Recently, the sub-continent slippers have emerged most prolific, clutching onto edges earned by spin-bowlers. Sri Lanka's demon slip Mahela Jayawardene caught 77 off Muttiah Muralitharan alone, the most common fielder-bowler out-caught dismissal in Tests. However, India's Rahul Dravid is top of the pile (not including wicketkeepers) with a total of 210 catches in Tests, the majority of them in the slips.

Left: Bucket hands: Australian master slip fielder Bobby Simpson catches England's Geoff Boycott off a Grahame Corling delivery during the first Test at Trent Bridge.

Right: South Africa's Jacques Kallis takes a catch in the cordon to get rid of Sri Lankan Thisara Perera at Kingsmead, Durban, in 2011. His sidekick A.B. De Villiers grins appreciatively.

1982

Bad Light

Frequently, bad light is in the eye of the beholder. Batsmen can spot a pin at 70 yards when victory beckons yet struggle to see past their nose when the ball is nipping about. The 1946–47 Ashes series in Australia was meant to be a friendly post-war get-together, but tempers frayed. According to the visitors, the umpiring was one-directional. And when Sid Barnes successfully appealed for bad light (eighth time of asking inside two overs), England's bowlers were apoplectic.

The wet pitch was a minefield and with an hour to stumps, they were confident of getting the top order cheaply. Barnes later admitted pulling a fast one, unashamedly having piled on 405 runs with Bradman the next day. However, England's own batsmen could see well enough to chase down 176 in 44 overs at a gloomy Karachi in 2000. As darkness fell, Pakistani captain Moin Khan tried to delay, winning himself no favours from umpire Steve Bucknor. Graham Thorpe and Graeme Hick combined for 91 precious runs as the fielders chased shadows. Five minutes later, the ground would have been pitch-black but Thorpe scrambled to earn a first Test triumph in Pakistan in 39 years.

Nowadays, umpires have sole control over bad light. Ironically, they are often criticized for being too sympathetic to batsmen, denying the paying public entertainment.

Left: Long-standing English umpire David Constant checks his light meter during the England v. Pakistan Test match in 1982.

Right: Good light starts play: the floodlights of the Sydney Cricket Ground attract spectators in their thousands to an evening Twenty20 match.

1968

Rain Stopped Play

The 1902 Ashes series was truly engrossing, showcasing one of Australia's finest touring sides. Even the best need luck, though. Skittled for their lowest-ever total of 36 in the first innings of the first Test at Edgbaston, thousands arrived the next day to watch England maul them in the second. Torrential rain turned the pitch into a marsh – match drawn. Australia eventually won the series 2-1.

In the days of timeless Tests (when the match lasted until one team won), the most famous was England v. South Africa (1939), which lasted until the tenth day. Remarkably, England were set to chase down the 696 runs needed for victory, but with 45 still needed, the heavens opened and a draw was declared for the visitors needed to sail back to Blighty. Not so timeless after all.

England's bid to level the 1968 Ashes series and retain the urn looked a damp squib when a thunderstorm struck the Oval on the fifth day, with five wickets still needed for victory. After the rain, hundreds of supporters poured onto the pitch to push away casual water and mop up puddles with towels, 'kerchiefs, sweaters – whatever it took. Derek Underwood was finally unleashed on the Aussie tail-end, taking the last wicket with just five minutes left. Would the umpires (or opposition captain) allow that nowadays?

Right: Spectators helped mop up the wicket after a flash storm threatened to deny England victory at The Oval in 1968. With just minutes to spare, Derek Underwood finally broke through John Inverarity's rearguard to level the series.

Far Right: A snapper takes shelter under a brolly at the Chinnaswamy Stadium in Banglalore, during a Champions' League Twenty20 match between the South Australian Redbacks and Somerset in 2011.

1961

Critical Run-Outs

Many a pavilion has borne the brunt of a needless run-out as the dismissed batsman lets rip behind closed doors. Occasionally he's unable to wait before revealing his deep-set frustration. In 1947, Australian Bill Brown was visibly irked when Indian bowler Vinoo Mankad ran him out for backing up too far. A bowler was expected to warn the non-striker, but Mankad dispensed with niceties and sent a steaming Brown on his way.

Derek Randall stormed back to the Trent Bridge pavilion in 1977 after Geoff Boycott called him through for an impossible quick single. The Nottinghamshire faithful were duly robbed of seeing their favourite son in top form. Boycott covered his face in shame before regaining his composure to score a hundred of his own. The following year, Boycott (now captain) was deliberately Shanghai'd by Ian Botham for scoring too slowly on instruction from vice-captain Bob Willis "to run the bugger out" – one order Botham joyously obeyed.

In 2005, Australian skipper Ricky Ponting publicly let fly at England's coach Duncan Fletcher after being caught short by substitute fielder Gary Pratt. In a match (and series) that England only just won, Ponting's premature end – well set on 48 – could have been the difference. Fletcher loved every insult!

Left: West Indian opener Conrad Hunte dives for the crease in vain, as Aussie keeper Wally Grout whips the bails off at Adelaide during the epic 1960–61 series. The visitors were eventually denied victory by a 110-minute last-wicket stand.

Right: Ricky Ponting storms back to the pavilion during the Trent Bridge Test of 2005, victim to a direct hit of substitute fielder Gary Pratt. The English fielders struggle to suppress their giggles in the background.

1970

Danger Zone

At what point does accurate, fast, short-pitched bowling cross over into intimidatory play that is contrary to the spirit of the game? Usually when someone gets hurt.

During the Bodyline series (Australia, 1932–33), the line was crossed. There are plenty who still defend Douglas Jardine's masterplan to stifle Don Bradman with "leg theory" – lots of fielders from leg slip to short-midwicket, and Harold Larwood bowling like the wind at the batsman's ribs and head. The Aussies were whining because the Poms were winning, they say.

On the other hand, this was totally pre-meditated and with malice aforethought, so much so that several English players refused to be party to it. Eventually it did injure a couple of Australian batsmen, notoriously Bert Oldfield, with a blow to the head that might have killed him. Oddly enough when the West Indies used the same tactics against England the following summer, leg theory was outlawed.

However, prolonged bouts of short stuff were legal in the late 1970s and 80s, when the West Indies' stable of thoroughbred quicks ruled Test cricket. Naturally, the bowlers did not want to hurt the batsmen but they were comfortable knowing that they probably would at some point. Several were injured, causing sustained "chin music" to be removed from the game.

Soft or sensible, you decide.

Right: Opener Geoff Boycott loses his cap to the first ball of his team's innings against Western Australia on a tour match in 1970. The bouncer, sent down by Dennis Lillee, grazed Boycott's forehead, but did not prevent him from scoring a ton.

Far Right: South African batsman Johan Botha retired hurt after a short ball from Ravi Rampaul ball burst through his helmet grill during a one-dayer against the West Indies in 2010. He returned to bat and ended up on the winning side.

Three
The Grounds

The spiritual home of the game – an aerial
view of Lord's Cricket Ground in 1946.

1895

Lord's Cricket Ground

It's little wonder that cricketers the world over dream of walking out onto the soft, lush turf of Lord's in London. From 1814, when a portion of Thomas Lord's grounds was given over to cricket, it assumed the role as spiritual home. The famous features have come a long way from the drained duck pond whose wicket was cut by grazing sheep, but the allure and charm remains.

W.G. Grace's brilliance was instrumental in establishing the ground's popularity for the MCC in the second half of the 19th century. Since the bearded doctor, remarkable performances by Bradman, Compton, Sobers, Richards, Botham, Hadlee and more recently Graeme Smith, Andrew Flintoff and Andrew Strauss have cemented its reputation as a showcase of talent. Graham Gooch holds the record for most runs (2015), most hundreds (6) and highest score (333 v. India in 1990), while the Australian bowlers have enjoyed their visits down the years, most famously Bob Massie's 16 wickets in 1972 and Glenn McGrath whenever he lined up an Englishman.

Then there's the terracotta pavilion, Long Room, Old Father Time, the space age Media Centre, the quirky slope, the Nursery, the Edrich, Compton and Mound stands, the Museum with its little urn – the list goes on and on. Lord's has achieved a rare blend of modern sports arena and authentic English tradition, which largely explains why its stands are full every summer.

Left: English public schools Eton and Harrow contest a match at Lord's in 1895. The ground's iconic Pavilion was less than five years old and cost £21,000 to build.

Right: More than 115 years on and the spectators' view from Lord's Edrich Stand (upper) – the Pavilion apart – is much changed.

1931

Scoreboards

The cricket scoreboard, so often the focus of a tight match, has evolved down the years into a mine of useful information. The glorious old manual versions are like a whirring grandfather clock, as pulleys, sprockets and levers are pushed and pulled to keep the spectators up to date, operated by invisible mice within. Electronic versions have largely replaced these mechanical beauties, of course giving maximum opportunity to flash up adverts between overs.

In one-day internationals, the matter starts to get tricky when rain dampens the occasion. The Duckworth/Lewis method kicks in, rejigging the score according to complicated algorithms and formulae. Its genius is that few fans – and least of all the commentators – know how it works, so we all just accept it as a workable solution.

Its predecessor failed spectacularly during the 1992 World Cup, when a tight run chase by South Africa was reduced to farce. Following a rain delay, the asking rate plummeted from 22 runs from 13 balls (with two set batsmen) to 22 runs from one ball.

In 2003, South Africa only had themselves to blame against Sri Lanka, as their management misread the D/L crib sheet. Wily old pro Mark Boucher, believing his team had enough run to win and progress from the group stages, blocked the last ball and punched the air in celebration. But the target on the graph was for the tie, not the win, which duly ejected the Proteas from their own tournament.

Right: A workman cleans the face of the huge scoreboard at the Hove cricket ground, Sussex, in 1931.

Far Right: The Old Trafford digital screen shows the situation with one ball left and England chasing one final wicket in the third Ashes Test in 2005. Australia's Brett Lee survived it to salvage a draw.

1961

The MCG

If Lord's is the home of cricket, the MCG is the beating heart with more than her share of raw drama. The Victorian passion for cricket galvanised the first England tours of Australia, culminating in the inaugural Test of 1877, won by the home side by 45 runs on the back of Charles Bannerman's brilliant 165 not out (out of 245). One hundred years later, Australia won by the same margin at the same venue.

Invariably, the MCG pitch is prepared to reward good cricket but the curator has no control over the crowds jamming into the bowl (up to 90,000 at a time). The acoustics send their collective thoughts down to the players, led by lager-fuelled larrikins in the infamous Bay 13 – a huge boost for the Australian who has done well and a wave of derision for the sorry Pom, having grassed a catch.

Don Bradman was imperious over 20 years, failing to score a hundred only once in a Test against England. Garfield Sobers' 254 for the Rest of the World in 1972 is hailed best of all time on Australian soil, while Dennis Lillee and Jeff Thomson's thunderous performance on Boxing Day gave new meaning to the word "Test". To beat the Aussies at the MCG is rare, but fulfilling for those who achieve it.

Left: A young fan watches the second Test between Australia and the West Indies from the top deck of the northern stand of the Melbourne Cricket Ground in 1961.

Right: Spectators watch day one of the fourth Test match between Australia and England at Melbourne Cricket Ground in December 2010.

1934

Stadium Advertising

Like squirrels round a picnic, stadium advertisers have become increasingly bolder, creeping ever closer until practically feeding from the hamper. Undoubtedly, the revenue they bring to the game – particularly through television – is invaluable but there's something endearing about the old black-and-white images of ovals surrounded by picket fences or just the crowds themselves.

First came the billboards, especially close to the scoreboard, advertising staples for the man of that time: paint, petrol, hair wax, maybe a meat pie in Australia … Boundary boards and title sponsors followed as Gillette gave impetus to one-day cricket in England and financial leader Prudential underpinned the fledgling World Cups. Cigarette companies (Wills, John Player, Benson & Hedges) have since been outlawed, but brewers such as VB, Castle, Foster's, Carib and Steinlager still wet the whistle of fans worldwide. Telecom giants (Vodafone, Cable & Wireless, 3 and Lebara) have emerged as corporate heavyweights, while motorbike and car companies compete to sponsor the subcontinent's Man of the Match.

Advertising has seeped into every available crack (stumps, sightscreens, drinks carts) – even the unglamorous umpires are walking banners. When a batsman acknowledges the crowd, his personal sponsor is lifted for the camera. Inevitably this leads the more cynical viewer to question loyalties. Nothing is beyond the reach of today's "Mad Men", it seems.

Left: Advertising for the *Daily Chronicle* at Headingley for the 1934 fourth Ashes Test.

Right: A contractor paints an advertising logo onto the grass at the Kensington Oval in Bridgetown, Barbados, in 2007.

1977

Eden Gardens

Kolkata's coliseum has changed immeasurably since rising to international recognition with its first Test against Douglas Jardine's touring side of 1934. In those days, Indian cricket was more English than the English; the original Gardens had a "garden" feel, with ladies in long dresses with parasols, gentlemen in vibrant blazers and polite applause for good play.

Nowadays, the crowds are colourful but a trifle more energetic, especially if the likes of Sachin Tendulkar or M.S. Dhoni are in full swing. With a capacity bordering on 90,000 emotional Bengalis, the ground has the least enviable reputation for rioting worldwide.

But for players and fans alike the huge concrete cradle is a pure celebration of the sport. Tests traditionally played around New Year demand an entry on the CV of every aspiring cricketer, who will count a century or five-for as a highlight. Some have risen to the challenge – Rohan Kanhai smashed 256 in 1959 to humble the home side. Others leave bewildered – Shane Warne was knocked about for 152 runs as V.V.S. Laxman and Rahul Dravid took India back from the brink in 2001, the greatest turnaround in Aussie fortunes since Botham in 1981.

With the arrival of the IPL carnival, the Eden Gardens have reached their zenith of seething, fizzing razzmatazz. For complete cricket sensory overload, visit Kolkata.

Left: An estimated 110,000 spectators pack in to see Derek Underwood bowl in the 1977 India v. England second Test. The official capacity was less, but there are ways of getting in.

Right: Praveen Kumar cuts a lonely figure in the outfield of Eden Gardens during an ODI against England in 2011.

1938

Technology

In 1929, Australia's captain Jack Ryder played his final hand for his country with a battling fifty to chase down a stiff fourth innings total. Had he failed, England would have won the Ashes 5-0. At a critical moment, the 40-year-old was run out by several feet with a direct hit.

"Not out!" boomed the umpire, to the fielders' clear annoyance. A quick check upstairs would have surely cooked Ryder's and Australia's geese. Should that belittle Ryder's achievement?

No, but it does beg the question how many other special knocks would have been ended prematurely by Hot Spot, Snicko, Hawk-Eye, Slo-Mo and the Decision Review System? Not enough, say the poor bowlers. That said, how many promising innings – and careers – were cut short without the chance for referral?

By and large, the system works better now. The end result is usually the right one, although happily there is still enough of a grey area on lbws to bring in the element of luck. Cricket wouldn't be a proper test if you didn't have to ride ill and good fortune. There remain teething problems with the availability of equipment (how can a batsman be in in one country, but out in another?), the role of captains and India's refusal to join the technological revolution, but there is more to celebrate than not.

Perhaps the greatest change has been the number of lbws awarded to spinners. A big stride is no longer a defence if that ball is going on to hit the stumps. The bowler given a fresh advantage? That will surely be turned over soon!

Left: Photographers use a long-focus camera from a rooftop at The Oval to capture images of Len Hutton's 364 against the Australians. The vicar used rather weaker lenses.

Right: A television camera man gets some sleep as he waits for play on day two of the first Test between Australia and India in 2003.

1925

Newlands

There are several iconic grounds in South Africa – the Wanderers in Johannesburg, for example, is a colossus of cricketing history – but Newlands' astonishing beauty steals the show. To sit in full view of Table Mountain and Devil's Peak, shaded by the gentle oaks where many of the finest bowlers and batsmen ply their trade, is to savour relaxation before a single ball is delivered. As the waft of brai drifts across deckchairs, you can't help but enjoy.

Exciting cricket is often the fare, notably in Tests where draws are uncommon. Indeed, in 1923, the touring MCC were pushed to the limit. With one wicket left and five needed to win, the ball soared toward the stands. Imagine the spectators' thoughts – a catch and South Africa win, six and England win, four and scores are tied. As it happened, the fielder just failed to catch the ball, it rolled over the boundary and England scrambled a single next ball to win.

South Africa's closest rivals in recent history have been the Australians, with some astonishing nail-biters leaving both sides scarred. In 2011 Australia were steamrolled for just 47 in their second innings and the home side quickly rattled off the necessary 236 to record a memorable win.

Naturally, the oaks didn't react, having seen it all before.

Right: Not so new: locals gather to watch a club match at Newlands Cricket Ground, Cape Town, in 1925. The setting feels more village green than international venue.

Far Right: In the shadow of Table Top Mountain, South Africa take on England in the third Test of the 2010 series. The home crowd were denied victory by a single wicket.

1977

Kensington Oval

The first stadium in the Caribbean to host a Test match in 1930 and venue for the 2007 ICC Cricket World Cup final, Bridgetown's Kensington Oval has assumed the status of ancestral home to the West Indies. Yet, close to the blue sea, with an enviable climate and charming atmosphere, Barbados sometimes feels like an away fixture for the home side as thousands of tourists flood through the turnstiles.

That earliest encounter with England brought out the best in the imperious George Headley, setting a reputation for a ground where good batsmen score runs and good bowlers take wickets. In other words, a fine wicket for Test cricket.

The whitest of white-knuckle rides came during a showdown between Brian Lara and Glenn McGrath in 1999, both tyros at the peak of their powers. Chasing 308 to win, Lara arrived at the crease with the score at 78 for 3. At 248 for 8, all seemed lost but Lara stared down the Aussies on a tumultuous final day. With help from tail-enders Curtly Ambrose and Courtney Walsh, he blazed his way to 153 not out as the West Indies won by one wicket. McGrath bowled brilliantly for 44 overs, took five wickets but left the arena a loser.

For those who rate Lara over Tendulkar, Bridgetown 1999 might be exhibit A in their argument.

Right: England captain Ian Botham scrutinises the grassy Kensington Oval pitch in 1981, on the brink of defeat. In the first innings, Michael Holding bowled a perfect over of hostile fast bowling to remove Geoff Boycott for a duck.

Far Right: Kensington Oval has undergone one of the most remarkable transformations of any major cricket ground. The wooden stands have gone and it now boasts a state-of-the-art media centre.

1981

The Dressing Room

The 'health' of the dressing room can play a telling role in the ability of a team to perform in the middle. What went on in the dressing room tended to stay there, but with the increase in biographies and social media, we hear about any mishaps sooner rather than later.

Don Bradman's "Invincibles", who plundered all of England in 1948, showed the power of a settled dressing room, although it did number some of the finest ever Australians. During the 1930s, in comparison, Bradman lacked the same warmth from team-mates Bill O'Reilly and Jack Fingleton, amongst others. No wonder he spent so much time in the middle…

Sometimes, tempers can overspill into confrontation. Before the 2007 ICC Twenty20 World Cup, Pakistan's speedster Shoaib Akthar was sent home after injuring fellow bowler Mohammed Asif with a flying cricket bat. Pakistan eventually lost the final to India by a whisker.

Many a window and light fitting has been broken by a batsmen piqued by an unfair or careless dismissal. During the 2011 World Cup, Ricky Ponting was ticked off by the ICC for smashing a TV after throwing his box across the room. Rock and roll!

The best solution, however, for all the rain delays, interminable batting partnerships and 12th man duties, is to sleep it off. England's Phil Tufnell was nicknamed "the Cat" on account of his ability to nap in any dressing room, no matter what was going on outside. Cricket's just a game – why take it all so seriously!

Right: England's Ian Botham smokes a cigar in the changing room after his match-turning 149 not out during the third Test match against Australia at Headingley in Leeds.

Far Right: Tubby or not to be: Mark Taylor, one of Australia's most successful captains, openers and slip fielders, takes off his pads for the last time in his professional career after a state match for New South Wales at the SCG in 1999.

1953

Vantage Points

Watching cricket can be an expensive business, so if you have the opportunity to see the action for free, a little discomfort or adventure is well worth the effort.

The buildings around the Kennington Oval in London are famous for their vantage points, which afford adequate views of the match below, albeit the privilege is usually reflected in the property price. Those that cannot gain access to balconies or window sills will risk life and limb atop chimney stacks and roofs (usually with a beer can in hand) in their determination to catch free sport.

At the old Recreation Ground in Antigua, fans would cling to trees overlooking the pitch, mindful not to celebrate wildly if their heroes prevailed. In India, where health and safety is sometimes an optional extra, every tree, grassy knoll or scaffold pole is fair game. The exit strategy is often an after-thought.

The corporate dollar has priced many of the true cricket fans out of the stadium, leading to frustrating scenes of empty seats and crowds in the streets. If the excluded find intrepid ways of finding free cricket, then who can blame them?

Left: Not to be denied: schoolboys – and adults – climb a high wall next to the distinctive gasometer and Oval Mansions to watch England take on the Australians in 1953.

Right: Indian fans find a vantage point on the scoreboard during the 2nd One Day International match between India and South Africa at the Captain Roop Singh Stadium in Gwalior in 1991.

Four
The People

Where would the game of cricket be without the crowd?
A sign exhorts spectators to "Hire a Cushion for Comfort,
Only 6d", during the England v. Australia Test match at
Headingley in 1930.

1948

Umpires

For years, the umpire was no more than a glorified bean counter. Occasionally he would venture a clear-cut decision but the two captains determined the field of play. Over time, control has been wrested away by officials – and a good thing, too.

Fearless Englishman Frank Chester (48 Tests, 1924–55) is credited with changing the balance of power. He was prepared to send the game's biggest names on their way if he thought it right. Mostly, he was right and the merits of this approach took root.

Dismissal is a dramatic affair, with the umpire sole juror and judge, although it has lost some of its finality with the review system. Twitchy Dickie Bird would aggressively waggle a finger to send a batsman on his way with a Barnsley "That's out!" Rudi Koertzen's "slow death" finger rise sent many to an early bath, while Steve Bucknor kept batsmen waiting for several excruciating seconds before pulling the trigger.

Former England Test umpire David Shepherd is fondly remembered for his superstition of lifting one leg in a jig on Nelson (111, 222, etc.) to avoid ill luck. But for sheer idiosyncrasy, with his trademark signals for six, four, drinks, tea – you name it – Kiwi official Billy Bowden rules. His crooked finger to give the batsman out surely disappoints and bemuses in equal measure.

Right: One of the great characters of the game, umpire Frank Chester taps his raised leg to signal a leg bye in 1948.

Far Right: Umpires Billy Bowden and Ian Gould send the players off due to bad light conditions in a Test between Australia and South Africa at Wanderers Stadium, Johannesburg, in 2011.

1914

Cricket Fans

In cricket's formative years, the viewing public were often seen as a frustration by noblemen seeking to play in private surroundings with a sense of exclusivity. Two hundred years on, fans are the lifeblood of the game, adding colour and vibrancy.

With the establishment of major grounds in the nineteenth century, crowds flocked to see the new game. So much so that pavilions, stands and refreshment stalls had to be built. Respectful, restrained and polite, cricketing fans revelled in the delights and complexities of the game still mainly played by the ruling classes.

Cricket has since gone from being an elitist sport to one open to all and naturally, the atmosphere has been transformed, from the cricket-obsessed Asian nations who dress up and create a carnival atmosphere to England's Barmy Army, able to celebrate even when their team is taking a pasting. Not everyone believes this to be a good thing: writer and commentator Christopher Martin-Jenkins once accused the Barmy Army of "demeaning English cricket".

Fan disaffection is not uncommon, from the merciless comments emanating from the Sydney Hill to unhappy Caribbean fans rioting after their star was omitted from a West Indies Test match, even Indian fans reacting so badly to a 1998 World Cup semi-final defeat that they caused the match to be abandoned.

Left: Play up! Play up! And play the game! Spectators are inches from the field of combat at Lord's in 1914 for a match on the public schools' circuit. With storm clouds gathering in Europe, the summer would prove the heyday for many of the young gentlemen.

Right: Sri Lankan cricket fans, sporting mohawk wigs and brandishing a lion mascot, bring added colour to their team's ICC Cricket World Cup match against Australia in 2011.

1907

Journalism

One good indication of how cricket reporting has changed beyond recognition was the reaction of the MCC in London to a telegram from the Australian Cricket Board in 1933, stating the England bowlers were acting in an unsportsmanlike manner with Bodyline tactics. The MCC replied to say they "deplored" the accusation and demanded it be withdrawn.

But the truth was they didn't know what it was about! Any news they received was based on the scorecards rather than the nature of play. While the papers Down Under were full of comment and leaks, all the MCC knew was that England were winning against the odds. To make matters worse, one of their primary sources was the recently retired Jack Hobbs, writing for *The Star*, who inevitably sided with former team-mates, leaving out the relevant juice. Nowadays, the MCC press office might have read Don Bradman's Twitter feed and not been so bullish.

Today's cricketers have no such freedom. In the 1930s, Freddie Flintoff and his pedalo would soon be forgotten. Two years ago the *News of the World* undercover scoop, which revealed the no-ball match-fixing scandal, went further in producing incriminating evidence. The details were splashed across the doomed Sunday tabloid, leading to the prosecution and incarceration of three Pakistani cricketers and giving "press charges" a whole new meaning.

Right: A special travelling Post Office telegraph van in use at Lord's for the between England and South Africa in 1907.

Far Right: Journalists work in the Lord's media centre during the ICC World Twenty20 match between New Zealand and South Africa in 2009.

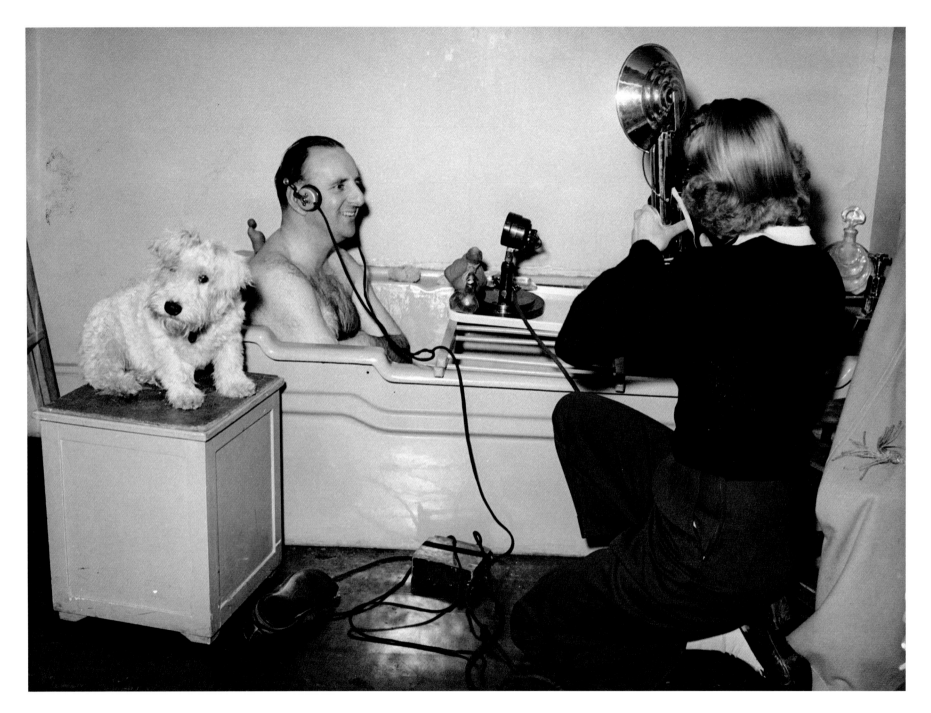

1952

Commentators

Cricket's radio glory days were probably the first 30 of the BBC's *Test Match Special*, which brought together the wide-ranging talents of John Arlott and then Brian Johnston.

Sombre, poignant, measured Arlott and playful, jolly, spontaneous Johnston might have jarred in other walks of life, but here they created a harmony that swept the public through the summer months and brought the four corners of the world into living rooms in winter. Naturally, they couldn't do it all on their own and attracted a host of other voices instantly recognisable down the airwaves: "CMJ", "Blowers", "Aggers", "Backers", "Bearders" … Who says only footballers come up with unimaginative nicknames?

The "leg-over" giggling fit between "Jonners" and Jonathan Agnew charmed those who had never previously warmed to cricket and remains a champagne moment in broadcasting. On TV, Richie Benaud was the face of cricket for several generations of Brits and Australians alike. His "Morning, everyone" and "Got 'im!" were mimicked across the globe.

Of course Benaud was an effective all-rounder but many of the above were professional journalists first, cricketers second. Today's commentary boxes are almost exclusively filled with former stars rising to the microphone as a rite of passage. You need 200 wickets or 5,000 runs to get a look in.

Left: Ever the professional, beloved cricket commentator Brian Johnston ignores the risks to broadcast from a bathtub in 1952.

Right: Laid-back cricketer turned laid-back TV presenter David Gower commentates as England take on Zimbabwe in 2000.

1956

Celebrities

Some cricketers have gone on to savour (or endure) celebrity status, but the sport traditionally struggles to project the same glamour as tennis or horseracing, perhaps because it's so male-dominated. In the 1930s, however, following the lead of ex-England-captain-turned-movie-actor C. Aubrey Smith, Hollywood founded its own cricket club comprising ex-pat enthusiasts such as Boris Karloff and P.G. Wodehouse. These extended garden parties attracted David Niven, Larry Olivier, Olivia de Havilland, Joan Fontaine and even icons like Cary Grant and Errol Flynn. Just how often they got their whites dirty is a moot point – rarely can cricket have seemed so debonair.

Aussie action men Russell Crowe and Mel Gibson have shown sword skills are transferable, padding up for a Hollywood Ashes tie against an England XI (Jude Law and Daniel Radcliffe, maybe not so tough?). Crowe at least had a genetic headstart (cousins Jeff and Martin were two of New Zealand's finest blades).

With the onset of T20, cricket enters a new era of extravagance as India's rich and famous rub shoulders with the biggest hitters. Bollywood starlets jiggle and beam after every big six and wicket, with some funding the action while politicians and tycoons compete for airtime. Every moment is captured on TV and processed by millions on Twitter or Facebook. So, sport or showbiz…?

Left: Pulling your leg? English comedians, including Tommy Cooper (in fez) and Norman Wisdom (batting) playing a charity cricket match at Sudbury, Middlesex, in aid of victims of cerebral palsy, in 1956.

Right: Hollywood actor Hugh Jackman gives one of his less polished performances against the leg-spin of Shane Warne in the MCG nets.

1956

Groundskeeping

In cricket's formative years, when grazing sheep mowed the pitch, the team who won the toss could choose the strip to bowl on, invariably one to suit their bowlers. By the turn of the twentieth century, petrol mowers and rollers took over and groundsmen got the hang of top dressing. Trent Bridge's curator, a certain Fiddler Walker, perfected the mix of Nottingham marl and manure to create batting paradises to all but guarantee longer matches, crammed with stroke-play and big centuries. Men like Jack Hobbs, Wally Hammond and Don Bradman filled their boots.

Of course it was bad luck on the bowlers, who had to hope for poor weather to gain any advantage. And it wasn't just England – one of the excuses given for Bodyline was that Australian pitches offered no assistance to conventional, high-class bowling. These marling techniques were largely outlawed after the War to bring more parity between bat and ball, but often led to a stalemate and "bore draws". Naturally, the host nation would prepare tracks to suit their best bowlers – dry and spinning (Chennai), green and swinging (early season Edgbaston), fast and fiery (Jamaica).

Recently, with the commercial incentive to host Tests that go the distance, or one-dayers where 300 chases 299, there's a return to batsmen-friendly pitches and once more, batting averages soar.

Right: England captain Peter May (left) and his Australian counterpart, Ian Johnson, inspect the wicket at Old Trafford prior to the fourth Test in 1956.

Far Right: The Lord's groundstaff remove the Hovercover from the wicket during one of the breaks for rain during a Pakistan v. Australia Test in July 2010.

1938

Coaches and Managers

Sir Pelham Warner, a fine batsman and journalist, won the dubious honour of managing England's Bodyline tour in 1932–33. The good-natured "Plum" adored travelling with the MCC as a player but was now embroiled in a storm that railed against his better nature.

Caught between deep hatred of Bodyline tactics and loyalty to England captain Douglas Jardine, Warner is said to have shed tears after Aussie skipper Bill Woodfull's stinging rebuke: "I don't want to see you, Mr Warner. There are two teams out there: one is playing cricket, the other is making no attempt to do so."

Fast-forward to 1996 and coach David Lloyd was no shrinking violet. Frustrated in its chase of 205 on the final afternoon in Zimbabwe, England eventually drew – with Nick Knight run out attempting the clincher. In the post-match press conference "Bumble" accused his hosts of delaying tactics before insisting: "We have flipping hammered them! One more ball and we'd have walked it. We murdered them and they know it!"

Possibly the defining moment of Lloyd's tenure, but he must be commended for bringing a more professional structure to the national squad, benefiting Duncan Fletcher and the current coach Andy Flower (who scored a hundred and completed the run-out). Did he ever dream he'd be sitting in Lloyd's seat, some 15 years later?

Left: Don Bradman with the Australian manager and two other members of the team watch their colleagues at practice amidst cricket gear strewn on the floor.

Right: Always room for improvement: Brian Lara is watched and filmed by West Indies manager Clive Lloyd (far right).

1935

Scoring

Happily, there is much more to cricket than the game itself. Hours go by without a lot going on, yet there's a pleasurable thrum to observation that gladdens the heart and calms the soul. For those fortunate enough to see cricket through this optimistic glass, no passage of play can ever be dull.

And for those who like to surrender themselves to cricket's biorhythms, there is scoring. These neat, efficient, fiercely territorial men and women immerse themselves in the match, recording every event as an artist captures a summer fair. Neither nerds nor geeks, they are gods: without them, chaos would reign.

The most famous are remembered as fondly as the best batsmen and bowlers. Australian Bill Ferguson pioneered the modern linear style of scoring, evolving bookkeeping from its most primitive state at the turn of the century. For more than 50 years, 41 tours and 204 Tests, the astonishing Ferguson acted as scorer and baggage-man for all the Test nations.

Another Bill, "Bearded Wonder" Frindall, was inspired by Ferguson as a teenager and eventually took over as scorer for the BBC in 1966, filling the shoes of Arthur Wrigley, who had held the post for 32 years. Frindall's encyclopaedic knowledge, kindly nature and beautifully crafted scorebooks made him a national treasure, beloved of *Test Match Special* commentators and listeners.

Right: The huge numbers of the scoreboard at Trent Bridge are rolled to show the score in the England v. South Africa Test Match in 1935.

Far Right: The scoreboard showing Australia all out for 47 runs against South Africa at Newlands in November 2011.

Five
The Culture

West Indian bowler Courtney Walsh takes shade behind an
advertising board on the field boundary during the fourth
Test match against England at Old Trafford in 1995.

1948

Training Days

Cricket often has a cruel sense of humour. The batsman who trains seven days a week, watches his diet, doesn't smoke or booze, gives himself the best chance of scoring lots of runs. But it's no guarantee that he won't nick off early and watch the fat lad, who rolled out of bed/the pub an hour earlier, smash a hundred.

Natural talent will win through over hard work. David Gower didn't get his sublime timing from shuttle runs and endless throw downs. Ian Botham gained an all-round game by bowling overs and batting in the middle, not the nets. Would he have caught more in the slips with today's reflex drills? Indeed, Inzamam-ul-Haq went into a form slump after he started a training regime.

Both England and Australia have made 'boot camps' part of their training culture, as much for the bonding benefits as the fitness. Aussie coach John Buchanan was given stick for organising a session in the outback prior to the 2006-07 Ashes, but they win the series 5-0.

With the advent of T20 cricket, training has needed to adapt to meet the new skills required for success. Batsmen will practice hitting sixes and undergo strength conditioning to beef the ball over the boundary. Bowlers, likewise, spend their time perfecting slower balls and yorkers.

Yet, for all that, we will always have Virender Sehwag, Jesse Ryder or Chris Gayle who have the pure talent to smash the ball on sight alone.

Left: Australian legend Don Bradman gives a batting lesson to Bill Brown before the fifth Test against India in 1948.

Right: Follow through: England's Graeme Swann gives team mate Stuart Broad tips on how to hit a big tyre with a mallet in 2011.

1921

The Toss

W.G. Grace is meant to have called "the lady" when tossing up. As the coins of his era had Queen Victoria on one side and Britannia on the other, he was a certain winner. He is also credited with saying: "When you win the toss – bat. If you are in doubt, think about it, then bat. If you have very big doubts, consult a colleague – then bat."

At Brisbane in 1954, the great Len Hutton won the toss and stuck the Aussies in ... then watched them bat for two and a half days, eventually passing 600. Ricky Ponting's brain fade during the 2005 Ashes crucially handed back the initiative to England after 16 years of easy dominance. Having won the first Test, Ponting opted to bowl first, despite losing strike bowler Glenn McGrath to a twisted ankle. England smacked 400 runs on that first day and started to believe.

Yet bowling first sometimes proves wise. Wily Sri Lankan Arjuna Ranatunga raised eyebrows when he asked England to bat first on a flat Oval track in 1998. But he knew that his trump card, Muttiah Muralitheran, must rest between innings; that wouldn't happen if England followed on. His plan worked perfectly, as Murali bowled England out cheaply second time around, taking 9 for 65 to secure a famous victory.

Right: Heads I win: Australian captain Warwick Armstrong and English captain Johnny Douglas at the toss-up before a Test match in 1921.

Far Right: Tails you lose: India's MS Dhoni (left) and Sri Lanka's Kumar Sangakkara agree to a re-toss of the coin after confusion ahead of the 2011 ICC World Cup final.

1937

Cricket Bats

The earliest cricket bats from the seventeenth and eighteenth centuries look more like hockey sticks than anything seen on the circuit nowadays, but they did roll the ball along the ground back then. By the mid-nineteenth century, with round-arm bowling firmly established, the familiar rectangular shape had evolved: willow emerged as the wood of choice.

"Touch" players such as Ranji, Victor Trumper, Jack Hobbs, Don Bradman, Wally Hammond, Len Hutton, Gary Sobers and their sort preferred lighter bats with thin edges for dabs, glides and late cuts. In the 1930s, Australian Bill Ponsford broke the mould with his "Big Bertha", weighing in at a meaty 2 lb 9 oz. Bats over 3 lb would become steadily more commonplace as batsmen sought power over precision.

Despite the odd scoop here and there, nothing really changed for 100 years. Bats were still durable (to use more than two a season was extravagant) and the scoring rate still steady. But all that changed with the advent of lightly pressed disposable bats. The modern blade is heavier and woodier than Ponsford's, yet feels as light and responsive as Hammond's, providing both power and touch. Better weight distribution and thicker edges send mishits for six. Indeed, batsmen who might have struggled 20 years ago have become modern-run machines.

Just imagine if Bradman had used a Kookaburra Kahuna …

Left: Two factory workers inspecting the 'Jack Hobbs' competition cricket bats in 1937.

Right: Australian captain Ricky Ponting (left) casts a discerning eye over teammate Michael Clarke's cricket bat during a practice session at the Sardar Patel Gujarat Stadium in Ahmedabad in 2011.

1924

Pitch Inspection

Often pitch inspection is a good indicator of a captain's mindset. More timorous captains tend to start looking for demons in the pitch otherwise ignored with a stronger batting line-up. England's Nasser Hussain famously inserted the Australians on the first day of the 2002–03 Ashes series in Brisbane and then watched delighted batsmen reach 364 for 2 by stumps on a motorway.

But as Geoffrey Boycott's car keys disappear into a crack or the pitch is tinged greener than Wimbledon's Centre Court, the inspection carries more weight. This was especially true on uncovered pitches. In 1894, Australia had dominated a timeless Test in Sydney, needing just 64 runs with eight wickets in hand at the end of the fifth day. England's beleaguered bowlers gathered in the pub to commiserate. But that night, a storm raged. After a cold shower to shake off his hangover, Yorkshireman Bobby Peel inspected the soggy wicket. The pitch was all but unplayable. "Gie me t' ball," he chuckled, before running through the Aussies to secure an ill-deserved victory.

Left: The South Africa and Leicester team captains expect the pitch in 1924. It was so bad that they decided to postpone the start of the match.

Right: New Zealand captain Daniel Vettori closely examines the pitch before the opening Test match against Sri Lanka at The Galle International Cricket Stadium in 2009.

1938

Drinks Break

Nowadays you are more likely to spot isotonic drinks bottles than teacups on the field of play. So, how on earth did they cope in the days before dieticians and sports scientists were part of cricket's touring caravan, before fitness regimes and abstinence were necessities?

Well enough, as it happens, albeit batsmen did not pinch singles or turn twos into threes, like they do today. But they still batted for days in the blazing heat. Water was for wimps, according to the old school.

Australian great Allan Border showed scant regard for personal hydration during a Test against India in 1986. When fellow batsman Dean Jones asked to retire, having scored 170 brave runs in 40 degrees and 80 percent humidity, his response was less than sympathetic. "You weak Victorian! I want a tough Australian out there, I want a Queenslander."

Jones went back out, reached his double hundred in a daze, fainted, then spent the next two days in hospital on a drip.

It was only the second time a Test was tied, as both teams were all out twice with the scores level. Everybody went a bit potty in that heat. Spinner Greg Matthews bowled unchanged for a whole day, sporting a sweater in a statement of defiance. And at the end of the madness, neither team won.

Left: Served in style, Don Bradman (seated) and the England fielders break for squash in a 1938 Test match against England at Headingley.

Right: More than 70 years on and the daintly served squash has been replaced by state-of-the-art energy drinks in plastic bottles. Here, Wasim Jaffer (right) and captain Rahul Dravid use the drinks break as an opportunity to refresh and talk tactics in 2006.

1933

Written Apologies

Cricket has always suffered a dual personality. Perceived as a noble and genteel sport, it can also be arena for all sorts of skullduggery as 22 players try to get away with whatever they can in pursuit of victory. Once the dust settles, the apologies begin in a bid to restore decorum.

All too often, politics demand that it's the cricketers who must apologise, even though they act with the tacit understanding of selectors and board. The wronged nation insists on seeing a famous sportsman dragged across the coals rather than the suits who are perfectly happy to shovel blame onto the player.

Fast bowler Harold Larwood, for example (who was Douglas Jardine's primary agent for the Bodyline antics of the 1930s) received precious little backing from the MCC. Indeed, he was hung out to dry and ordered to sign a confession that he had organised the whole sorry escapade. Upon refusal, he didn't play for England again.

After his finger-wagging spat with Pakistani umpire Shakoor Rana, Mike Gatting was forced to take the blame and apologise so that the tour could continue and relations between England and Pakistan did not deteriorate further. His hastily scribbled apology on a napkin did the job, but again begged the question: should cricketers really have to get involved in international horse-trading?

Right: Australia's Bill Woodfull ducks to avoid a rising ball from England's Harold Larwood during the fourth Test match at Brisbane on the infamous "Bodyline" Tour in 1933. Larwood refused to take the blame for the controversy.

Far Right: During the heated second Test at Faisalabad in 1987, England captain Mike Gatting has it out with Pakistan umpire Shakoor Rana. Gatting was made to apologise, which he did on a napkin.

1994

Ball Tampering

Cricketers have always looked for any advantage they can get away with, legal or otherwise. For many, it's dirty linen best not aired.

In theory, only natural substances like sweat and saliva may be used to shine the ball, hence the hoo-ha in Chennai in 1977, when India's captain Bishen Bedi – under pressure having lost the Series – accused England's John Lever of shining the ball with Vaseline.

The grease had been applied to Lever's forehead to stop sweat pouring into his eyes – unsuccessfully, it transpired. But when Bedi found Vaseline-soaked gauze in the outfield, he complained. Lever, who had spearheaded England's win, was branded a cheat despite precious little proof. Bedi eventually apologised but the mud had already stuck.

When it was their man in the dock – megastar Sachin Tendulkar, no less – the Indians were equally vociferous. In 2001, camerawork clearly showed the Little Master working the seam with his fingers, which led to Scottish referee Mike Denness awarding a suspended one-match ban.

The charge was cleaning the ball without informing the umpire – Denness never said Tendulkar had tampered with the seam or shape – but the Indian cricket board interpreted this as an accusation of cheating, fuelled by racism. Denness was duly scapegoated as the Indians flexed considerable financial muscle.

Right: Michael Atherton examines the ball during the fifth Test at The Oval against South Africa in 1994, where Devon Malcolm took nine wickets in the second innings. At Lord's, Atherton had caused a stink by drying the ball with dirt from his pocket.

Far Right: Umpires Darrell Hair (holding the ball) and Billy Doctrove inspect it with Inzamam-ul-Haq of Pakistan at The Oval in 2006. After being accused of ball tampering Pakistan refused to return to the field and the Test match became the first one ever to be ruled a forfeit.

1993

Sledging

Most sledging comprises plain old trash-talking. It tends to be the off-the-cuff retorts that enter folklore. Waist size and wives are inevitably popular topics for debate. "How's your wife, and my kids?" was a famous opening shot from Rod Marsh to Ian Botham. "The wife's fine, but the kids are retarded," came the speedy reply.

Such playground humour earned immortality for burly pace bowler Eddo Brandes. It bears repeating. "Why are you so fat, Brandes?" added Australian fast bowler Glenn McGrath after the Zimbabwean chicken farmer had played and missed several times. "'Cos every time I make love to your wife, she gives me a biscuit."

Shane Warne loved to chirp, especially when he knew the batsman couldn't pick him. South Africa's Daryll Cullinan was one of his favourite "bunnies" and he once greeted him to the crease with "I've been waiting for two years for another chance to humiliate you."

"Looks like you've spent it eating," replied Cullinan, quick as a flash.

There are some batsmen who revel in the confrontation. Fielding captains would often tell their players to stay quiet when Viv Richards or Brian Lara came to the crease, rather than rile them into feats of brilliance.

Glamorgan bowler Greg Thomas made the mistake of piquing Viv during a County match in Cardiff, after beating the Antiguan several times in the same over. "It's red, round, weighs about five ounces, and you're supposed to hit it," he said helpfully.

The next delivery ended up in the river Taff. "Greg, you know what it looks like. Now go find it."

Right: Mike Atherton grins at Merv Hughes during the 1993 Ashes Test match at Lord's. Hughes doesn't grin back, but would have the last laugh when his throw left Atherton sprawling short of his crease on 99.

Far Right: England's Alan Mullally tunes in to Steve Waugh's 'mental disintegration' tactics. Not often the fast bowler is chirped by the batsman!

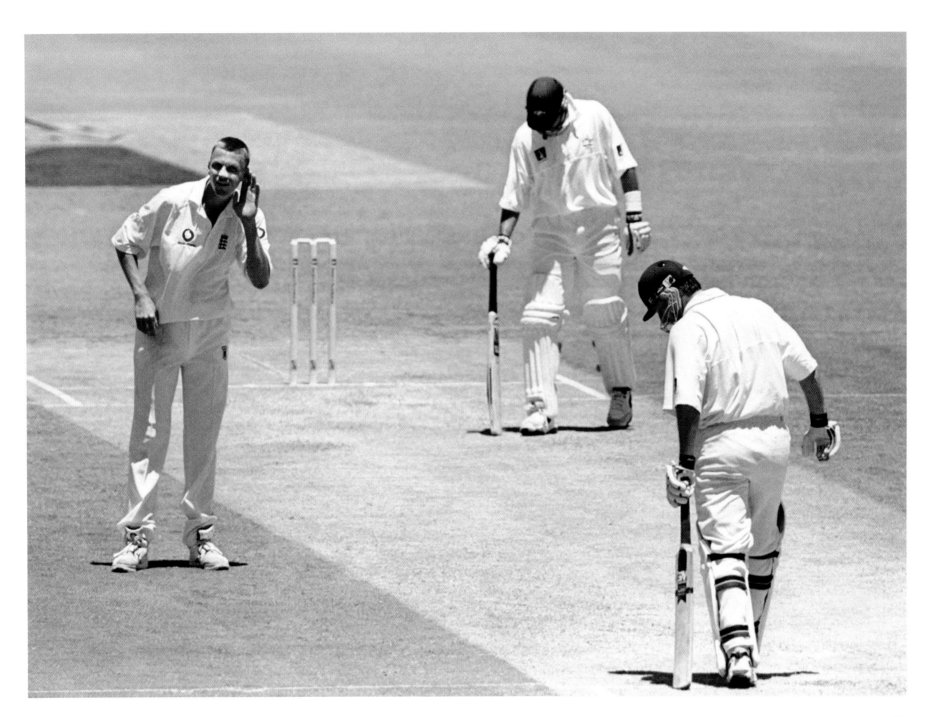

1973

Invasions

The image of crowds running onto the pitch to throng their idols is mostly consigned to nostalgia as the threat of more sinister forces has forced a ring of security until the players have left. But pitch invasions were once the norm: often the final two batsmen at the crease had to sprint for the pavilion if they wanted to leave the field in possession of pads, gloves and bat.

When India drew level in their chase of England's 213 at Old Trafford (1983), fans prematurely flooded the pitch. Defeat inevitable, England captain Bob Willis stacked his fielders on one side so they could make an escape. He himself lobbed the last delivery and was running off the pitch before it reached Kapil Dev.

West Indian crowds are also fond of impromptu stampedes but local exuberance once cost them the match. In a tight one-dayer against Australia (1999), Steve Waugh needed three to win off the last ball. The Guyanan crowd saw him bunt it to long on, presumed victory, so poured onto the pitch. All six stumps were removed by the time the ball made it back to the bowler, while both batsmen were obstructed from attempting a second, let alone a third.

The West Indies would probably have won, but the referee astutely declared a tie.

Left: England wicket-keeper Alan Knott (right) and Graham Roope watch as pitch-invading fans congratulate Clive Lloyd on scoring a century on the first day of the first Test between England and the West Indies at The Oval in 1973.

Right: Pakistan's Saqlain Mushtaq waits for the third umpire's decision on his run out as the crowd invade the pitch in the game against Bangladesh in the ICC Cricket World Cup in 1999.

1976

Crowd Trouble

Bodyline's shenanigans would not be the last time an England fast bowler caused Aussie crowds to froth. At the Sydney Cricket Ground in 1971, fiery seamer John Snow hit Terry Jenner on the head, forcing the tail-ender off injured. Jenner was collateral damage in an ongoing battle between Snow and Australian umpire Lou Rowan, whose opinions on the definition of intimidatory bowling differed considerably. England were also aggrieved that in five previous matches not one Australian batsman had been given out lbw.

Rowan cautioned Snow for the Jenner delivery, with the crowd booing and hollering before hurling pies and cans at Snow when he retired to the third-man boundary between overs. One drunk even tried to grab him. England skipper Ray Illingworth marched his men off the pitch in an unprecedented act that might have forfeited the match and the Ashes. Instead they returned to regain the urn.

The Eden Gardens also boast some of the most passionate fans – and how they love a good riot! 1996 proved an ignominious episode in the nation's history, as Sri Lanka reduced India to 120 for 9 from 98 for 1 in the World Cup semi-final. Riled supporters set alight sections of stadium and scattered the field with bottles and fruit. Referee Clive Lloyd eventually awarded Sri Lanka the match.

Right: Umpire Bill Alley attempts to "stump" the West Indian supporters during the invasion of the pitch after the West Indies' convincing victory over England in the final Test of the 1976 series.

Far Right: Stewards break up crowd trouble during the ICC Champions Trophy semi-final between West Indies and Pakistan at The Rose Bowl, Hampshire, in 2004.

1938

Sportsmanship

W.G. Grace made a great performance out of being a gentleman when clearly neither an amateur nor a bastion of fair play. Indeed, after he ran out Australian Sammy Jones in 1882, fast bowler Fred Spofforth was so incensed that he bowled England out for next to nothing – a collapse leading to the creation of the Ashes rivalry.

When winning at any cost becomes key, inevitably the greatest losers are the paying spectators. There are those who maintain Greg Chappell's decision to make his brother Trevor bowl underarm against the New Zealanders in 1981 was canny, being within the laws of the day. New Zealand needed a six to tie, so the pea-roller guaranteed victory. Any defenders form a tiny minority: fans, commentators and even prime ministers decried it as a crime against the spirit of their beloved sport.

Sri Lankan spinner Suresh Randiv was similarly vilified in 2010, when reprimanded for bowling a no-ball to Virender Sehwag, denying him a hundred. The scores tied, Sehwag needed a single to score his thirteenth ODI hundred – a wonderful effort chasing just 170 runs for victory. He clubbed the no-ball out of the ground but according to the laws, the extra run took precedence and Sehwag was stranded on 99. Randiv apologized, but the offence remains on his record.

Right: English cricketer Len Hutton is congratulated by Don Bradman and the Australian team when he made the world record Test score of 364 at The Oval in 1938.

Far Right: Andrew Flintoff consoles Brett Lee after England defeated Australia at Edgbaston in the second Ashes Test match in 2005.

1975

Controversy

Ideally, sportspeople should never be dragged into political wrangling but public life is not so straightforward. Basil D'Oliveira (1931–2011) was thrust into a maelstrom in 1968, when picked for the upcoming tour of South Africa. But South Africa's Apartheid government declared they would not allow the naturalised "Cape coloured" all-rounder to play. England duly withdrew, forcing South Africa into sporting isolation until the early nineties. Tenacious and courageous on the field, "Dolly" won admirers worldwide for the dignity and integrity he displayed throughout.

By 2003 South Africa were well and truly back in the international fold, hosting the showpiece Cricket World Cup. If only they had staged it entirely at home, the tournament might have remained on the back pages. Instead, when England drew to play in Zimbabwe – mid-collapse under Robert Mugabe's brutal regime – the players grew concerned about death threats and refused to participate. With no intervention from the Foreign Office, the decision to boycott the match (and forfeit points that in all likelihood cost them their place in the latter stages) was left to captain Nasser Hussain and the ECB.

How can a captain concentrate on a small, round, fast-moving object and lead his country to glory, while making snap diplomatic decisions that could well jeopardise his players' security?

Left: The captains of England and Australia, Tony Greig and Ian Chappell (left) looking at the wicket which had been vandalised overnight by oil at Headingley in 1975 in protest at the arrest of London robber George Davis.

Right: The *News of the World's* headline was prescribed reading for MCC members during the England v. Pakistan Test match at Lord's in August 2010.

1975

Injuries

Helmets have removed some risk of serious injury, albeit many more are hit on the head than before sporting them became common practice. Indian left-hander Nari Contractor was one of the gutsiest batsmen but he got it wrong against Barbados' lightning-fast Charlie Griffith in 1962. Ducking into a bouncer that hit him on the back of the head, he was fortunate to survive. Tragedy was averted after players from both sides donated blood.

A helmet proved no protection for Mike Gatting's nose in a one-day international in 1986, when Malcolm Marshall skidded one through his defences in Kingston. The ball, which ricocheted down onto the stumps, had bone shards studding the leather. Two years later, West Indian Phil Simmons was on the receiving end of some English pace, crowned by a bouncer from David Lawrence. Batting sans helmet, Simmons nearly cashed in his chips as his heart stopped on the way to the hospital. Within a few seasons, he was bashing English bowlers round the park again.

Justin Langer was one of Australia's toughest competitors but even he was forced from the pitch in 2006, when South African speedster Makhaya Ntini sconed him with the first ball of the match. Langer's hundredth Test was over inside two seconds. Without a helmet, he might have been permanently dismissed.

Left: Sri Lankan batsman Duleep Mendis is carried from the field after being struck on the head by a bouncer bowled by Australia's Jeff Thomson during the a 1975 World Cup match at The Oval. Australia won by 52 runs.

Right: Steve Waugh (near) and Jason Gillespie make for a sorry sight in a Sri Lankan hospital after their bone-breaking collision under a high catch in 1999. To add insult to injury, the catch was dropped and Sri Lanka easily won the match.

1938

Diet and Fitness

Cricket has long enjoyed a reputation for being a sport in which fitness and athleticism are bonuses, not prerequisites. It's certainly the case at English village level, where an iced bun earns the same appreciative murmurs as a caressed cover drive or a deceptive googly. The old-fashioned belief that you'll only get properly fit through playing has plenty of supporting evidence, too. Bowlers like Larwood, Lindwall, Statham and Trueman, who built up their endurance by bowling overs, resembled thoroughbred horses. Larwood apparently would enjoy a pint and a cigarette in intervals; Bradman's ability to bat for days was not achieved counting calories.

The temptation is strong to insist that modern cricketers, with their weight training, VO2 max shuttle runs, nutritionists, ice baths, psychologists and isotonic drinks, are barking up the wrong tree. Yet the game has altered from even 15 years ago. Sheer volume of matches, plus the importance placed on fielding and running between wickets, means players are expected to operate full throttle at all times, whether Test or T20.

There is the occasional throwback – like Virender Sehwag or Chris Gayle – who succeed without showing too much exertion. England's Samit Patel, however, must surely wish he played in a different era – when value was calculated in runs and wickets, not pounds and inches.

Left: Warwickshire cricketers leaping over a bench in 1938, in the days when players got fit by playing and ice baths were filled with beer bottles.

Right: The advent of one-day cricket has improved players' fitness and pre-match routines as shown by Muttiah Muralitharan's (left) back-stretching exercise with Suraj Randiv.

1975

Bizarre Interruptions

It's not always rain or bad light that stops play. Animals – dogs with short legs, cows at cow corner, the occasional pigeon on a death mission – have all interrupted the flow of a cricket match.

But the creature that has earned cricket most notoriety is the common or garden streaker. Given the vast majority of spectators at a cricket match are men with a couple of drinks to their name, a female streaker will attract more appreciation than a male.

In 1989, Sheila Nicholls caused a stir when she cartwheeled naked across the sacred turf of Lord's, gaining the front and back pages of several nationals for good measure. Her performance did her little harm, sparking a successful singing career.

Male streakers tend to receive less sympathy. In 1977, Greg Chappell took the law into his own hands, giving one invader a beating with his bat. His teammate Terry Alderman dislocated his shoulder, tackling a drunken Englishman during a heated Ashes Test match at Perth's WACA in 1982.

Aussie glory seeker Robert Ogilvie got more than he bargained for, when he ran past Andrew Symonds during a tight run chase at the Gabba in 2008. Symonds, who was built like a blindside flanker, took him out with a well-timed shoulder barge, sending Ogilvie sprawling.

Symonds was quickly exonerated.

Right: Streaker Michael Angelow hurdles the stumps at Lord's in 1975, as England's Allan Knott grins at the other end. The Navy cook was fined £10, the same amount his mates had bet him to do it.

Far Right: Seagulls fly past as the West Indies opener Chris Gayle prepares to face an Australian delivery in 2009.

1932

Tours

In the days before long-haul flights, a cricket tour was more a career sabbatical than a sporting break. Ashes tours could last six months, about three of them on the boat. Many of the best amateurs refused to travel so the visiting team was often lacking in true strength. The bandwagon might be more of a travelling circus show than a crack squad of athletes, providing an excuse for gentlemen to adventure in the colonies. Several enjoyed it so much, they never sailed home; others found homesickness and constant displacement made life a misery.

A tour of India was traditionally seen as the greatest test of unity and resolve. Oppressive heat, humidity, teeming crowds and almost inevitable illness could drain the most talented tourers. England's eccentric wicketkeeper Jack Russell would bring his own teabags and cereal, while Shane Warne shipped over his favourite baked beans, so avoiding the dreaded "Delhi belly".

The antics and temptations of 30 men away from home have doubtless remained the same down the decades. What's changed is that the old adage "what goes on tour, stays on tour" has been replaced by "what goes on tour, turns up in the Sunday papers". If today's team managers (or wives, for that matter) want to check if their charges have strayed, they follow the Twitter feed.

Right: Australian players chat to the media on the Southampton dockside after sailing halfway around the world for their 1932 tour of England.

Far Right: Shaun Pollock (left) and Mark Boucher push their luggage trolleys through Karachi International airport in 2007. Pakistan deployed dozens of police officers including elite commandos as the South African cricket team arrived for a month-long tour of the country.

169

1929

Cricketing Wives

The first WAGs (or CWAGs in cricketing circles) were perhaps the members of White Heather – the first ladies' playing club, formed in Yorkshire in 1887. Many of these pioneers were snapped up by England's ruling elite, most notably star all-rounder Lucy Ridsdale, who married future prime minister Stanley Baldwin.

Batsman John Edrich wedded US tennis star Pat Stewart, albeit briefly, though she did at least appear at one Wimbledon as Mrs J.H. Edrich. The Nawab of Pataudi, the Muslim captain of India in 1969, caused a stir in marrying Hindu beauty Sharmila Tagore, the first Bollywood actress to appear onscreen in a bikini. Imran Khan, likewise, caused tittering in tying the knot with the attractive daughter of tycoon Sir James Goldsmith, Jemima.

Australia's gossip pages of 2010 went into overdrive when golden couple Michael Clarke and supermodel Lara Bingle announced the end of their engagement. Clarke has bounced back pretty well, assuming to the captaincy and scoring a bundle of runs in the process. Away from cricket, Clarke has a new partner, ex-Miss Australia and former swimwear model Kyly Boldy. But the big celebrity match is the upcoming nuptials of Shane Warne and British actress Liz Hurley (she of the safety-pin dress and Austin Powers fame). The pair's rock-solid partnership has defied expectation despite the media glare. Good luck to them!

Left: Mr & Mrs Jack Hobbs could travel almost with without harassment, especially on a cross-channel ferry, even though he was England's pre-eminent player.

Right: Shane Warne and Liz Hurley attract crowds of fans and paparazzi travelling alone. Now that they are going out together, privacy is almost impossible.

1925

Trappings of Success

Original "shamateur" W.G. Grace made a mint, although given the entry fee doubled with his appearance, perhaps deservedly so. Adonis C.B. Fry was so highly regarded as the quintessential English gentleman that the Albanian government apparently offered him its throne. One wonders how the fortunes of the Balkans might have changed, had cricket become an obsession. Yet Fry turned it down because it came with a price tag: £10,000 annually.

Benefit years and testimonials represent an opportunity for cricketers to build a war chest for their retirement years. Naturally, some find it easier than others. In 1948, 94,000 packed into the MCG to watch Bradman score 123 in his testimonial. Shortly afterwards he was knighted by the British government for services to cricket.

Oddly, perhaps, Bradman remains the sole Australian to be knighted (the West Indies have seven), although his Bodyline series captain – Bill Woodfull – refused. Shane Warne (who may yet be knighted) made great play of the fact that every member of the English squad who won the 2005 Ashes received an MBE, including Paul Collingwood, who played one Test, scoring 17 runs.

Where Fry fell short, Ashley Giles (MBE) succeeded. In his testimonial year, he commissioned several thousand mugs printed with "King of Spin". A misspelling returned them as "King of Spain" – an instantly more valuable over-claim.

Left: In winter months, professional cricketers would have to work for a living, but the only very best, such as Jack Hobbs, would be able to combine work and play. An buzzing crowd gathers outside the window of Jack Hobbs' shop in Fleet Street, London, in 1925.

Right: Modern superstars have a management team to make decisions that allow them to concentrate on cricket and make life to be as easy as possible. Today's top cricketers can also reap considerable fortunes as shown here by Kevin Pietersen as he leaves training in his Ferrari.

1985

Celebrations

Cricket's two most important trophies could not be more different, yet both are among the highest points in a player's career. The terracotta urn is nothing much to look at, containing remnants of a burned bail or piece of rag, yet hundreds of Englishmen and Australians have pushed body and nerves to breaking point to regain or retain it. It has sparked diplomatic controversy, fame and fortune, deep enmity and lasting friendship. One or two nearly died in its pursuit – but who wouldn't swap all playing memories for the chance to hit an Ashes hundred or bowl one's team to eternal glory?

Of course, it's not just the Ashes. Showdowns between the top teams lead to memorable series – Test or one-day internationals. Domestic trophies and increasingly, domestic T20 tournaments, rate highly on any CV. But one need only witness the boyish excitement of Sachin Tendulkar, a batsman who has achieved so much, to realise what it meant to lift the 2010 ICC World Cup. A match-winning performance such as this guarantees a hallowed place in history.

How reassuring, in a game so driven by personal wealth and commercialism, that the old-fashioned draw of collective success and national pride still counts for plenty. Perhaps, after all, cricket has not changed so much between yesterday and today.

Left: Allan Lamb (far left) and Paul Downton (far right) watch Mike Gatting and Ian Botham spray skipper David Gower, who is about to celebrate England's 1985 Ashes win with champagne.

Right: Sachin Tendulkar is arguably the most beloved player in Indian cricket history and that love knew no bounds after his country won the 2011 ICC World Cup.

1939

Meeting the Public

It's tempting to believe cricket matches were once more crowd-friendly. Players seemed more accessible, less aloof somehow. During intervals, children frolicked on the pitch, stewards never body-searched; bouncers never ring-fenced boundaries in high-viz jackets. Surely it's just nostalgia, though? One of cricket's enduring charms is that players are still exposed to the public by the very nature of an open-plan pitch and spectators' proximity. Between deliveries, the boundary fielder can exchange autographs and banter with wags behind him.

Naturally, this sometimes leads to over-exposure as tempers fray. Pakistan's Inzamam-ul-Haq infamously motioned for a new bat in Toronto, though he was fielding at the time. Upon its arrival, he waded into the crowd to assault a spectator who had been tormenting him all day with a megaphone. Like Eric Cantona's karate kick, Inzi received both admonishment and sympathy.

For India's megastars, the public represents a daily challenge. After all, if Sachin Tendulkar wanted to walk from one end of Mumbai to the other, it would take several weeks (and changes of clothes) to get through his adoring crowds. He is forced to live in a guarded complex and relishes anonymity abroad. Mahendra Singh Dhoni attracts hoards to admire his haircut, sparking an instant trend to rival Cheryl Cole or Jennifer Aniston. Happily, Kevin Pietersen's "racoon chic" didn't catch on so fast.

Right: West Indies opener J.B. Stollmeyer takes time to sign an autograph for a deferential youngster at Old Trafford in 1939.

Far Right: In February 2008, South African all-rounder Shaun Pollock retired, and fans weren't backward in wanting a signed memento from his final match.

1981

High Jinx

One man's harmless fun is another's irresponsible act of stupidity. Perhaps the most infamous episode unfolded in the skies above the Gold Coast on the 1990–91 Ashes tour (England were thrashed). David Gower had been one of the bright lights, scoring two hundreds, but the team under Graham Gooch were two-down and low on morale. Midway through a first-class match against Queensland, Gower and fellow batsman John Morris – both already dismissed – attempted to lift the mood.

As their rented Tiger Moth biplane buzzed over the Carrara Oval, Allan Lamb pretended to gun it down with his bat from the crease, well aware who was flying above. It might have been written off as japery, but the management saw differently. When Gower's form dipped, he was controversially left out of the next squad to India; Morris never played for England again.

In the 2007 World Cup, England's poor showing was deemed a reflection of lynchpin Andrew Flintoff's off-field antics. According to press reports, a drunken Freddie had to be rescued from a pedalo off the coast of St Lucia. England subsequently bombed out – one theory being the squad was so well behaved after "Fredalo", they were too uptight to perform. Or perhaps the truth is, you can get away with practically anything… so long as you're winning.

Left: Bosom buddies: England's Geoff Boycott receives a kiss from team-mate and captain Ian Botham during their Tour to the West Indies in 1981.

Right: England's celebrations after winning the Ashes in 2005 were excessive, but after 18 years, Michael Vaughan (far left), Kevin Pietersen et al were forgiven.

1940

The Cricket Ball

Compared to many aspects of the game, the four-piece stitched leather ball with its cork centre has stayed much the same for several hundred years. The cottage industry of nimble seamsters – famously in Tunbridge Wells, Kent – has been almost entirely replaced by machining factories in the sub-continent, but the ball's composition and performance has changed only marginally down the years.

The advent of day-night, limited-over cricket witnessed the introduction of white balls against a black sightscreen. Teething problems meant that in certain conditions the ball could swing almost around corners; this could result in teams being blown away in one-sided contests or bowlers struggling to deliver six straight balls in ten. Much of that early swing has gone, leading to ferocious onslaughts in the early powerplays. And as soon as bowlers developed the skills to reverse-swing the old ball, the decision came to bring a new, clean pill after 35 overs – just in time for the final powerplay. Who says it's not a batsman's game?

Both white and red balls may be for the scrapheap, if the pink pioneers perfect their art. In theory, this compromise would replicate the consistency of a red ball but bring the visibility of a clean white one. In other words, the best of both worlds – unless it seizes too many wickets …

Right: Cricket ball manufacture is still a laborious task and, in 1940, the cork cores were hand-hung to dry before being wound with cotton and covered in leather.

Far Right: At the MB bat and ball factory in Sialkot, Pakistan, the final part of the process involves hand polishing the balls to bring out the shine.

OFFICERS MESS CIGARETTES

WITH COMPLIMENTS

FROM THE PROPRIETORS

ENGLISH TEAM 1909-1910 ON BOARD S.S. SAXON.

1909

Endorsements

Traditionally eclipsed by footballers, English cricketers were relegated to local radio ads and opportunistic product placement with some notable exceptions. The most famous being the late, great Denis Compton, whose filmstar looks and debonair attitude made him perfect for the face of Brylcreem.

"Compo" would have been a tabloid editor's dream and a team manager's nightmare but in the 1950s public life was far less open, allowing his prodigious talent as a batsman to blossom alongside an appetite for fine wines and finer women. In Compton, Brylcreem discovered the ultimate pin-up: women wanted to have him, while men wanted to be him.

Ian Botham also attracted suitors, whether as one half of Beefy and Lamby (Allan Lamb), or as living proof that Shredded Wheat is good for the heart. More recently we've learned that Andrew Flintoff shops in supermarkets, Kevin Pietersen wears watches and Alastair Cook drinks bottled water but they all pale into insignificance compared to Indian cricketing superstars. Sachin Tendulkar was first to make the move but even he has made way for the pulling power of Mahendra Singh Dhoni. Tendulkar's $38 million contract of 2006 was overhauled in 2010, when the amiable captain-wicketkeeper-batsman-heartthrob signed a deal worth $42 million, including endorsements for 22 products. And that was before he powered India to World Cup glory …

Left: A 1909 cigarette packet showing the England team en-route to South Africa on board *S.S. Saxon.*

Right: Sachin Tendulkar's image was probably on as many billboards around India in the 1990s and 2000s as any Bollywood star.

1929

Caps and Hats

No country takes its headwear more seriously than the Australians, who get doe-eyed at the mention of their Baggy Green Cap. Since the turn of the last century, Aussie players have all sported the celebrated cap, although it hasn't always carried today's hallowed importance. Bradman was a devotee, but the Chappell brothers chose comfort over conformity.

Mark Taylor performed the re-brand, decreeing every new cap be ceremonially presented (usually by an ex-player). Steve Waugh took the ritual still further, insisting a player had just one Baggy Green for life with the inevitable result that his own became slightly dog-eared by the end. Ricky Ponting has been criticized for looking like a tramp in his "daggy" green; even denigrating the prestige of the cap, though rarely has there been a prouder wearer.

The wide-brimmed maroon West Indian hat is another icon of proud identity. Flamboyant batsman Richie Richardson sported the canvas halo long into the era of helmets, scoring plenty of runs in the process. He would have little sympathy for English all-rounder Chris Lewis, who suffered sunstroke after fielding bareheaded during a West Indian tour. Scorched by the 'Prat Without A Hat' headline in *The Sun* newspaper, Lewis had just shaved his head before taking to the field … then sitting the rest of the match out in disgrace.

Right: Modern japes: cricketers in Devon in 1929 impersonate the old style cricketers of the Victorian era in top hats.

Far Right: England's Jack Russell finds some shade durring net practice in Bendigo in 1995. Russell used to prepare for playing in hotter climes by spending time in saunas wearing his full wicket-keeper's kit.

1978

Wearing a Lid

The first form of protective headgear in cricket was introduced by the popular player Patsy Hendren, who was second only to Sir Jack Hobbs' 199 for most first-class hundreds (170). The English player sported a three-peaked cap padded with sponge rubber, lovingly fashioned by his wife in 1933 to ward off the bumper barrage from West Indian pace men Manny Martindale and Learie Constantine. Somehow the idea took a while to catch on. More than 40 years, in fact, until speed merchants such as Andy Roberts, Michael Holding, Joel Garner, Dennis Lillee, Jeff Thomson and Bob Willis were sticking it up batsmen, time and again. Not everyone had the pain threshold of Brian Close …

Englishman Dennis Amiss wore one in the World Series Cricket, before Australia's eccentric Graham Yallop was the first to sport a helmet in a Test – against the West Indies' Roberts, Colin Croft and Garner in 1978. Resembling traffic cops in outer space, both players were repeatedly ridiculed for their pioneering spirit.

Soon, however, those who didn't wear protection – Viv Richards and Richie Richardson among them – stood out more than players who did. Today's "lids" are becoming increasingly streamlined: Sri Lankan ace Kumar Sangakkara looks as if he is setting off on a bike ride rather than plundering another double hundred.

No doubt Patsy Hendren's devoted spouse would heartily approve.

Right: Graham Yallop (with motorbike helmet) and Graeme Wood (without) prepare to face the West Indian music at Bridgetown in the 1977–78 tour.

Far Right: Andrew Strauss top edges the ball into his helmet grille during the final day of the Lord's Test against New Zealand in 2004. On debut, Strauss hit a century in the first innings, but was denied his second when run out by Nasser Hussain.

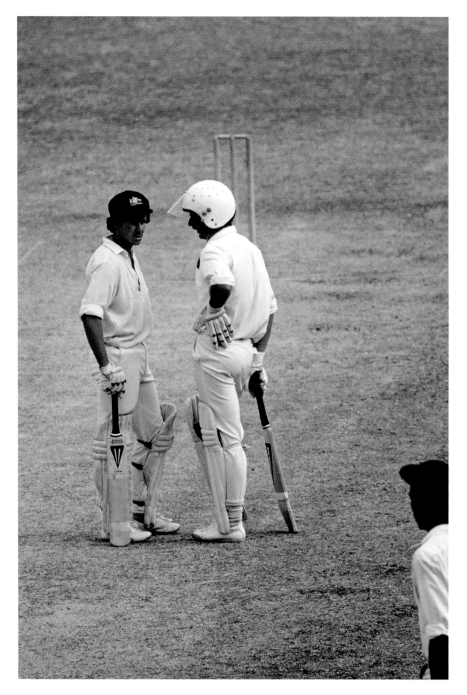

1972

The Cricket Day Out

If you dropped a cricket spectator from the 1930s into a modern stadium, then he might take a while to acclimatise.

There would be the extra noise, for a start. Impromptu music between overs used to be the preserve of West Indian venues, but now most grounds will blare out uplifting tunes to keep the crowd buoyant. Visiting Asian fans, especially, add to the atmosphere with their own horns and drums, which hit fever pitch when one of their heroes reaches a landmark with the bat or takes a wicket.

Throughout England's Ashes drought in the 1990s and early 2000s, their travelling supporters enjoyed marked success as the Barmy Army, (mostly) endearing themselves to local crowds. With a talented trumpeter, and a medley of both amusing and jingoistic songs, this group of indomitable merry-makers kept English spirits up despite the on-field woes.

The advent of T20 and the IPL has brought cricket closer to the razzmatazz of US sports, in particular the cheerleaders and pre-match divas. The shorter, glitzier format has offered a lifeline to English county or state teams that struggled to attract members to the first class or even 50-over matches.

For perhaps the first time since pre-television days, cricket grounds have enjoyed sell out crowds. Although does it really matter that not everyone is there for the cricket? Of course not.

Left: A day's cricket lasts for hours and fans need to eat and drink, even rock legends such as Rolling Stones frontman Mick Jagger, at The Oval in 1972.

Right: Australian fans form an illicit 'beer snake', made from empty beer cups on 'The Hill' at the Adelaide Oval cricket ground in 2006.

1981

Friendships

The game of cricket certainly throws up moments of fierce rivalry and intense bitterness on the pitch. This usually blows over once the stumps are drawn, although the odd rumbling feud can sometimes emerge. Mostly, however, cricket is too slow and informal a game to build any lasting grudges – indeed quite the opposite often occurs as opponents get to know one another, build up respect and so become lifelong friends.

In the aftermath of the Second World War, it was perhaps understandably hard to take cricket too seriously. England and Australia's two best players, Denis Compton and Keith Miller, were determined to keep their sport in perspective, enjoying themselves on (and especially off) the pitch. This shared attitude resulted in years of friendship, which have since been immortalized by the Compton–Miller Medal – now awarded to the best player in an Ashes series. Indeed, Miller even named his son after his friend.

County cricket often led to mixed loyalties, for overseas players would find themselves up against their fellow English pros in Test matches. Ian Botham and Viv Richards soon became great mates, spearheading Somerset to glory alongside Joel Garner. Imagine those three on song together! When the county controversially sacked the two overseas players in 1986, Botham decided to leave the team in a mark of solidarity.

Right: County colleagues Ian Botham and Viv Richards put the world to right during the 1981 series in the West Indies. Viv wears a T-shirt in support of Guyana's refusal to host their Test on the grounds that Robin Jackman – who had previously worked in Apartheid South Africa – had been picked to play by England,

Far Right: Opposing captains Shane Warne and Sachin Tendulkar embrace before the coin toss ahead of the 2010 Indian Premier League match between Rajasthan Royals and Mumbai Indians played at Sawai Mansingh Stadium, Jaipur.

Picture Credits

Ready and waiting: Australian cricketers (left to right) Rick McCosker, Doug Walters, Greg Chappell and Ian Chappell wait for a chance at Edgbaston in 1975.